THE CARTOON GUIDE TO LAW

Also available by Douglas Michael

THE CARTOON GUIDE TO ECONOMICS

THE CARTOON GUIDE TO
LAW

Douglas Michael

BARNES & NOBLE BOOKS

A DIVISION OF HARPER & ROW, PUBLISHERS

New York, Cambridge, Philadelphia, Washington

San Francisco, London, Mexico City, São Paulo, Singapore, Sydney

FIRST EDITION

Library of Congress Cataloging-in-Publication Data

Michael, Douglas.
  The cartoon guide to law.

  Bibliography: p.
  Includes index.
  1. Law—United States—Caricatures and cartoons.   I. Title
KF387.M53   1987   349.73'0207   85-45215
ISBN 0-06-460422-5 (pbk.) 347.300207

87 88 89 90 91 MPC 10 9 8 7 6 5 4 3 2 1

CONTENTS

AS SOMEONE ONCE SAID...

THERE ARE LAWS...

AND THEN, THERE ARE LAWS!

AND THEN... OF COURSE... THERE ARE MORE LAWS...

AND EVER MORE LAWS...

THERE IS NO DENYING THAT LAWS GOVERN EVERY ASPECT OF OUR LIVES. UNDERSTANDING LAW AND THE JUDICIAL PROCESS IS ESSENTIAL FOR US ALL. THE PURPOSE OF THIS BOOK IS TO FAMILIARIZE YOU WITH BASIC TERMINOLOGY AND PROCEDURE IN THOSE AREAS OF THE LAW YOU ARE MOST LIKELY TO ENCOUNTER.

THE FIRST THING TO UNDERSTAND ABOUT LAW IS HOW IT IS ADMINISTERED. IN ORDER TO WORK WELL, THE JUDICIAL SYSTEM IS BROKEN DOWN INTO VARIOUS CATEGORIES. FOR EXAMPLE: TAX COURT, TRAFFIC COURT AND CRIMINAL COURT ARE THREE SEPARATE CATEGORIES OF LAW. THIS SPECIALIZATION OF LAW IS RELATIVELY NEW. DURING THE FRONTIER DAYS OF THIS COUNTRY JUSTICE WAS USUALLY DISPENSED BY WHAT WERE CALLED "CIRCUIT RIDERS." THESE WERE JUDGES THAT RODE ON HORSEBACK FROM TOWN TO TOWN SETTLING ANY DISPUTE THAT WAS BROUGHT BEFORE THEM.

JURISDICTION

JURISDICTION IS TO A COURTROOM WHAT ZIP CODE IS TO THE POST OFFICE. JURISDICTION NOT ONLY INDICATES WHAT TYPE OF CASE A PARTICULAR COURT WILL TRY BUT ALSO SPECIFIES WHAT GEO-GRAPHICAL AREAS A COURT HAS AUTHORITY OVER. THESE GEOGRAPHICAL BOUNDARIES ARE DETER-MINED BY POLITICAL BOUNDARIES. THUS, SOME COURTS HAVE JURISDICTION OVER A CITY, OTHERS OVER A COUNTY. EACH STATE HAS ITS OWN COURT SYSTEM. AND, OF COURSE, THE FEDERAL GOVERNMENT HAS COURTS THAT HAVE JURISDICTION IN VARIOUS DISTRICTS OR REGIONS OF THE COUNTRY AS WELL AS THE SUPREME COURT, WHOSE INTERPRETATION OF THE LAW HAS JURISDICTION OVER ALL OTHER COURT-ROOMS IN THE COUNTRY.

HIGHEST COURT IN THE LAND

JURISDICTION
ORIGINAL → APPELLATE

ONE MORE DISTINCTION OF THE TERM "JURIS-
DICTION" MUST BE MADE. THERE ARE, IN OUR
JUDICIAL SYSTEM, COURTS OF ORIGINAL
JURISDICTION AND COURTS OF APPEAL, OR APPELLATE
JURISDICTION. A COURT OF ORIGINAL JURISDIC-
TION IS ANY COURT THAT HEARS A CASE FOR
THE FIRST TIME AND RENDERS A DECISION.
SHOULD THE LOSING PARTY FEEL THAT THE
DECISION IS WRONG, HE MAY APPEAL THE
CASE TO AN APPELLATE COURT. THE
APPELLATE COURT WILL NOT RE-TRY THE
CASE. HOWEVER, IT WILL REVIEW THE
CASE THROUGH RECORDS, TESTIMONY AND
BRIEFS GIVEN AT THE FIRST TRIAL.
THE APPELLATE COURT WILL THEN SUSTAIN
(APPROVE) OR DENY THE APPEAL. IF THE
APPEAL IS APPROVED, THE APPELLATE
COURT WILL REVERSE THE DECISION OF
THE LOWER COURT AND MAY ORDER
THAT A NEW TRIAL BE HELD.

APPELLATE COURT.

PLAY IT AGAIN, SAM,
ONLY THIS TIME
GET IT RIGHT.

COMITY

THE COURT SYSTEM OF EACH STATE IS SIMILIAR IN STRUCTURE TO THAT OF THE FEDERAL COURT SYSTEM. THUS, THERE ARE STATE COURTS OF ORIGINAL JURISDICTION AND STATE APPELLATE COURTS, AND EACH STATE EVEN HAS ITS OWN SUPREME COURT. FOR THIS REASON, STATES DO NOT ALWAYS CONFORM IN THEIR INTERPRETATION OF THEIR LAWS. FOR EXAMPLE, SOME STATES PERMIT MINORS TO MARRY WHILE OTHERS DO NOT. THEREFORE, TWO MINORS WHO LEGALLY WED IN TEXAS MAY REMAIN MAN AND WIFE SHOULD THEY MOVE TO IOWA, A STATE THAT DOES NOT PERMIT MINORS TO WED. THIS RESPECT FOR STATE AUTONOMY IS CALLED COMITY, WHICH IS ANOTHER WORD FOR COURTESY.

WELL SURE, TEX, WE'LL TAKE 'EM... AS A COMMON COMITY TO YOUR FINE STATE.

LEGAL PROCEDURE

THERE ARE TWO WAYS TO ENTER THE LEGAL SYSTEM. A PERSON ACCUSED OF BREAKING THE LAW ENTERS THROUGH THE CRIMINAL JUSTICE SYSTEM, AND A PERSON WHO IS SUED OR SUES ANOTHER ENTERS THROUGH THE CIVIL COURT SYSTEM. EITHER WAY THE LEGAL PROCEDURE IS ROUGHLY THE SAME AND IS GENERALLY UNIFORM IN ALL FIFTY STATES.

CASE STUDY

TO ILLUSTRATE THE BASIC LEGAL PROCEDURE, LET'S LOOK AT THE CASE OF NORTON CULP.

ONE DAY, NORTON CULP WAS EN ROUTE FROM THE DIPPY TWIN ICE CREAM PARLOUR TO HIS HOME

A DOG (IDENTITY UNKNOWN) DID DART IN FRONT OF MR. CULP'S AUTO AS HE WAS PROCEEDING IN A LEGAL MANNER.

OVERHEAD VIEW

MR. CULP'S CAR MARKED "A"

THIS UNEXPECTED ACTION CAUSED MR. CULP TO VIGOROUSLY SPLAY HIS ICE CREAM ACROSS HIS FACE, GREATLY REDUCING HIS FIELD OF VISION, THUS IT WAS THAT HE PROCEEDED IN A RECKLESS AND HAPHAZARD MANNER ACROSS THE CENTER LANE.

IT SO HAPPENED THAT A MR. ED FLAM HAD JUST NEGOTIATED A VERY TIGHT AND TESTY PARALLEL PARKING SPACE AND WAS FISHING FOR COINS BESIDE THE METER WHEN DESTINY, IN THE VANILLAED FACE OF NORTON CULP, CAME HEADLONG INTO HIS AUTO, GREATLY ALTERING ITS SIZE AND SHAPE.

CRASH

FIRST TO ARRIVE ON THE SCENE WAS PATROLMAN PETE DRISCOLL. OFFICER DRISCOLL FILED AN ACCIDENT REPORT, WHICH CITED MR. CULP FOR OPERATING A VEHICLE IN A RECKLESS MANNER. HE ALSO FELT COMPELLED TO ISSUE MR. FLAM A PARKING CITATION AFTER MR. FLAM STEADFASTLY REFUSED TO PLACE A COIN IN THE EXPIRED METER.

DETAIL OF THE ACCIDENT REPORT AS RENDERED BY PATROLMAN PETE DRISCOLL.

A - MR. CULP
B - MR FLAM

TRAFFIC COURT

MS. SCHUM

FACED WITH A SERIOUS CITATION (RECKLESS OP.) MR. CULP HIRED MS. SCHUM, AN ATTORNEY AND ACQUAINTANCE OF HIS BROTHER-IN-LAW. TOGETHER THEY ENTERED COURT AND PLEADED GUILTY, WITH MITIGATING CIRCUMSTANCES.

JUDGE HOLBIEN

WHIMSICAL JUDGE HOLBIEN, UPON HEARING THE CIRCUMSTANCES RESULTING IN THE ACCIDENT, RECALLED HIS YOUTH AND THE DAY HIS DOG SPUNKER MET UP WITH A DRIVER SOMEWHAT LESS CONSCIENTIOUS THAN MR. CULP. THE JUDGE FOUND MR. CULP GUILTY AS CHARGED BUT SUSPENDED ALL COSTS AND FINES, THEN CALLED A HALF-HOUR RECESS BEFORE HEARING ANY MORE CASES THAT DAY.

NOW FOR THE BAD NEWS

CULP

UPON RETURNING HOME FROM WHAT MR. CULP CONSIDERED A TRIUMPHANT MORNING IN COURT, HE WAS MORE THAN DISHEARTENED TO BE HANDED A SUMMONS TO ANSWER A CIVIL SUIT FROM MR. FLAM. BUT WHAT BOWLED HIM OVER WAS A NOTICE FROM HIS INSURANCE COMPANY THAT NOT ONLY REFUSED HIS CLAIM BUT REFUSED TO PAY ANY CLAIMS AT ALL BECAUSE HIS POLICY HAD EXPIRED OVER SIX MONTHS AGO.

WHEN MR. CULP CALLED MS. SCHUM OVER, SHE READ THE COMPLAINT THAT ACCOMPANIED THE SUMMONS AND SPECIFIED THE DAMAGES.

"MR. FLAM SEEKS $4000.00 FOR DAMAGES TO HIS CAR. $30.00 FOR A PARKING CITATION AND $30,000.00 FOR PAIN AND SUFFERING."

"WHOOA!"

FACED WITH A HEFTY LAWSUIT, MR. CULP AGREES TO RETAIN MS. SCHUM AS HIS ATTORNEY. MS. SCHUM IMMEDIATELY REQUESTED MR. FLAM'S ATTORNEY TO PROVIDE A BILL OF PARTICULARS. THIS WOULD PROVIDE MS. SCHUM WITH MORE SPECIFIC INFORMATION REGARDING THE DAMAGES.

"PLEASE, MR. CULP, TRY TO RELAX... $30,000.00 DOESN'T SOUND REALISTIC TO ME. CHANCES ARE THE ACTUAL FIGURE WILL BE MUCH CLOSER TO $25,000.00"

BILL of PARTICULARS

ON EXAMINING THE BILL OF PARTICULARS, MS. SCHUM NOTED THAT THE PAIN AND SUFFERING CLAIMED BY MR. FLAM RESULTED DIRECTLY FROM HIS BEING TICKETED BY PATROLMAN DRISCOLL AND ONLY INDIRECTLY FROM MR. CULP'S HAVING RESHAPED MR. FLAM'S CAR.

10

AT THIS POINT ATTORNEY SCHUM CONSIDERED FILING A DEMURRER. THIS IS A LEGAL DOCUMENT THAT DOES NOT DENY THE COMPLAINT BUT SEEKS TO INVALIDATE IT FOR A VARIETY OF POSSIBLE OF REASONS. IN MR. CULP'S CASE, MS. SCHUM THOUGHT A DEMURRER POSSIBLE SINCE THE 'DAMAGES THAT MR. FLAM CLAIMED WERE CAUSED BY PATROLMAN DRISCOLL'S HIGH SENSE OF DUTY AND NOT DIRECTLY BY MR. CULP'S AUTO ACCIDENT.

APPEARING BEFORE THE TRIAL JUDGE, MS. SCHUM AND MR. PLOTZ (MR. FLAM'S ATTORNEY) AGREED THAT MR. CULP WAS ONLY PARTLY TO BLAME FOR MR. FLAM'S SEVERE BODY TICS, SUDDEN GESTICULATIONS AND NUMEROUS OTHER SUFFERINGS. AND AS SUCH MS. SCHUM'S DEMURRER WAS DENIED.

LATER, MS. SCHUM AND MR. PLOTZ IMBIBED AT A NEARBY PUB, WHERE MS. SCHUM LEARNED THAT MR. FLAM WAS DEAD-SET ON TAKING THE SUIT TO TRIAL FOR REASONS THAT MR. PLOTZ WAS UNABLE TO FATHOM

11

WHEN MR. FLAM MADE IT CLEAR THAT HE WANTED THE CASE TO GO TO TRIAL, MS. SCHUM HAD TO TAKE DEPOSITIONS, OR PRE-TRIAL TESTIMONY, FROM THE PLAINTIFF (MR. FLAM) AND THE WITNESS (PATROLMAN).

MR. FLAM →

"WHAT IS THIS ALL ABOUT? I WANT MY DAY IN COURT. THAT'S WHAT THIS IS ALL ABOUT."

"DARN RIGHT. I WANT A JURY TRIAL!"

"I CAN'T CONTROL THIS SORT OF THING. SEE THAT?"

PATROLMAN DRISCOLL →

"I CITED THE DRIVER OF CAR 'A' FOR RECKLESS OP. THEN I CITED CAR 'B' FOR AN EXPIRED METER."

"WHEN I GAVE HIM THE PARKING TICKET, HE THOUGHT I WAS KIDDING. BUT IT WAS NO JOKE. HE PROCEEDED TO FLY INTO A RAGE."

Q. "BUT DON'T YOU THINK IT WAS AN INAPPROPRIATE TIME TO TICKET THE MAN'S CAR? AFTER ALL..."

"JUSTICE IS BLIND, MA'AM."

THE NEXT STEP THEN WAS TO SCHEDULE A DATE ON THE COURT CALENDAR. ONCE THIS WAS ARRANGED, BOTH LITIGANTS WOULD PICK A JURY. TO DO THIS BOTH SIDES WOULD TRY TO FIND TWELVE CITIZENS WHO THEY FELT WERE FAIR AND IMPARTIAL.

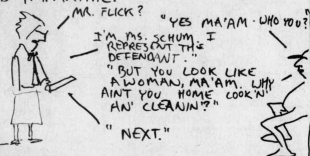

MR. FLICK? "YES MA'AM. WHO YOU?"

I'M MS. SCHUM. I REPRESENT THE DEFENDANT."

"BUT YOU LOOK LIKE A WOMAN, MA'AM. WHY AIN'T YOU HOME COOK'N' AN' CLEANIN'?"

"NEXT."

ONCE THE JURY WAS SELECTED, THE CASE WENT TO TRIAL.

THE COURTROOM

1. THE JUDGE. IN A JURY TRIAL HE INSTRUCTS THE JURY AND GUIDES THE TRIAL. IN A NON-JURY TRIAL HE ALSO RENDERS THE VERDICT.

2. THE WITNESS STAND. WHERE TESTIMONY IS GIVEN UNDER OATH.

3. THE JURY BOX. WHERE THE JURY OBSERVES THE TRIAL.

4. THE PLAINTIFF/PROSECUTOR TABLE.

5. THE DEFENDANT/DEFENSE TABLE.

6. THE BAILIFF. HE ADMINISTERS THE OATH TO ALL WHO ARE TO OFFER TESTIMONY. HE IS ALSO THERE TO ASSIST THE JUDGE AND ENFORCE HIS WISHES.

7. THE COURT STENOGRAPHER. THIS PERSON RECORDS THE PROCEEDINGS OF THE TRIAL.

TRIAL PROCEEDINGS

START →

AS COUNSEL FOR THE PLAINTIFF, MR. PLOTZ MADE HIS OPENING STATEMENT TO THE JURY.

"LADIES AND GENTS...IF I MAY CALL YOU THAT"

IN HIS OPENING STATEMENT, MR. PLOTZ OUTLINED HIS CASE AND THE BASIS FOR HIS CLIENT'S COMPLAINT. HE ALSO STATED HOW HE INTENDED TO PROVE THE DEFENDANT LIABLE.

"YEAH...SEE, I HAVE NO CONTROL OVER THIS SORT OF THING."

MR. PLOTZ WAS THE FIRST TO CALL WITNESSES TO THE STAND. HE CALLED MR. FLAM AND ASKED HIM TO DEMONSTRATE HIS DISORDER TO THE JURY.

IT WAS NOW MS. SCHUM'S TURN AS DEFENSE COUNSEL TO MAKE HER OPENING STATEMENT OUTLINING HER DEFENSE.

WHEN HE WAS FINISHED, MS. SCHUM WAS ALLOWED A CHANCE TO CROSS-EXAMINE THE WITNESS.

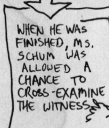

"YOUR WITNESS, PATTY, ER, UH." MS. SCHUM.

MS. SCHUM SET OUT TO DEMONSTRATE TO THE JURY THAT MR. FLAM WAS QUICK-TEMPERED.

"MR. FLAM, DID YOU DRIVE TO COURT THIS MORNING?"

"WHY, I'D LIKE TO KILL SOMEONE WITH MY BARE HANDS."

"A THIRTY-DOLLAR TICKET... HOW DO YOU FEEL ABOUT THAT, MR. FLAM?"

"WHAT?"

"WHY YES, WHY?"

"DID YOU PUT A COIN IN THE METER?"

"OF COURSE."

"THEN YOU WERE NOT AWARE THAT YOUR METER HAD EXPIRED AND THAT YOU HAD GOTTEN A TICKET?"

AS MS. SCHUM HAD HOPED, MR. FLAM FLEW INTO A RAGE AND WAS DRAGGED FROM THE COURTROOM BY THE BAILIFF. SHE THEN SHOWED THE ALLEGED TICKET TO THE JURY—A LAUNDRY RECEIPT. CALLING MR. FLAM A RAVING LUNATIC, SHE QUICKLY MOVED FOR A DISMISSAL OF THE CASE.

"ALL RIGHT THEN, CASE DISMISSED."

WHEN MS. SCHUM CALLED FOR A DISMISSAL, THE JUDGE ASKED HER AND MR. PLOTZ TO APPROACH THE BENCH. THE THREE STRUCK A DEAL WHEREBY MR. CULP AGREED TO PAY ALL DAMAGES TO MR. FLAM'S CAR AND BE FOUND FREE FROM LIABILITY TO MR. FLAM'S ALLEGED PAIN & SUFFERING.

HAD THE TRIAL CONTINUED, MS. SCHUM WOULD HAVE BEEN GIVEN AN OPPORTUNITY TO CALL WITNESSES TO THE STAND WHOM MR. PLOTZ COULD THEN CROSS-EXAMINE. ONCE ALL EVIDENCE AND TESTIMONY HAD BEEN PRESENTED, MR. PLOTZ WOULD HAVE SUMMED UP HIS CASE TO THE JURY. MS. SCHUM WOULD HAVE DONE THE SAME, MAKING HER CLOSING ARGUMENT. THE JUDGE WOULD THEN HAVE INSTRUCTED THE JURY AS TO THEIR DUTY IN REACHING A VERDICT. THE JUDGE WOULD THEN HAVE RELEASED THE JURY FROM THE COURTROOM TO DELIBERATE. WHEN THE JURY REACHED THEIR VERDICT THEY WOULD HAVE RETURNED TO THE COURTROOM TO ANNOUNCE THEIR DECISION. THE JUDGE WOULD THEN HAVE DETERMINED THE DAMAGES ACCORDINGLY.

CHAPTER TWO

CONTRACTS

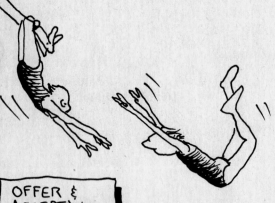

OFFER &
ACCEPTANCE

CONTRACTS ARE LEGAL OBLIGATIONS.
CONTRACTS ARE CREATED WHENEVER WE AGREE WITH
ANOTHER TO PERFORM OR ACCEPT SOME SERVICE
OR DELIVER GOODS.

"I CINDERELLA, IN EXCHANGE FOR A
HORSE-DRAWN CARRIAGE, DRESS, GLASS SLIPPERS
AND A TICKET TO THE BALL, HEREBY
AGREE TO BE HOME BY THE STROKE OF TWELVE...
SOUNDS FAIR; WHERE DO I SIGN, FAIRY GODMOTHER?"

WE ACT IN ACCORDANCE WITH SOME
FORM OF CONTRACTUAL OBLIGATION NEARLY
EVERY MINUTE OF EVERY DAY. THE FAILURE
OF ONE PERSON OR PARTY TO PERFORM
A CONTRACTUAL OBLIGATION MAY BE CON-
SIDERED A BREACH OF CONTRACT. THE
CONSEQUENCES OF A BREACH OF CONTRACT
ARE SELDOM PRETTY AND OFTEN END UP
IN A COURTROOM.

TYPES OF CONTRACTS

- EXPRESS -

AN EXPRESS CONTRACT IS NOT NECESSARILY A NON-STOP CONTRACT. IT IS RATHER A CONTRACT IN WHICH THE TERMS HAVE BEEN SPELLED OUT (USUALLY ON PAPER) AND AGREED TO BY BOTH SIDES.

- IMPLIED -

UNLIKE AN EXPRESS CONTRACT, AN IMPLIED CONTRACT IS ONE IN WHICH A LEGAL CONTRACTURAL BASIS IS RECOGNIZED INFORMALLY BASED ON THE ACTIONS, BEHAVIOR OR PAST PERFORMANCE OF ONE OR BOTH PARTIES.

WHERE ARE YOU TAKING ME? I SAID KENNEDY AIRPORT!

SO! I DONT FEEL LIKE GOING TO KENNEDY. I FEEL LIKE GOING TO CONEY ISLAND.

WAIT A MINUTE. YOU'RE A CABBY. THIS IS A CAB. I HAILED YOU. YOU PICKED ME UP. YOU HAVE TO TAKE ME WHERE I WANT TO GO... WE HAVE AN IMPLIED CONTRACT.

TAXI

- UNILATERAL -

A UNILATERAL CONTRACT IS A CONDITIONAL CONTRACT. THAT IS, THE CONTRACT IS ONLY BINDING IF THE CONDITIONS OF THE CONTRACT ARE MET.

- BILATERAL -

A BILATERAL CONTRACT IS ONE IN WHICH BOTH PARTIES MAKE PROMISES TO EACH OTHER. FAILURE OF EITHER PARTY TO FULFILL THEIR CONDITION MAY RESULT IN A BREACH OF CONTRACT FOR WHICH DAMAGES MAY BE SOUGHT.

EXECUTED - EXECUTORY

AN EXECUTED CONTRACT IS A CONTRACT THAT HAS BEEN CARRIED OUT FULLY BY BOTH PARTIES. AN EXECUTORY CONTRACT HAS YET TO BE COMPLETED BY EITHER OR BOTH PARTIES.

- VOID -

VOID CONTRACTS ARE BAD FROM THE START. THEY ARE IN SOME WAY ILLEGAL AND THEY ARE NOT ENFORCEABLE IN COURT.

"SAY... THERE'S SOMETHING ROTTEN ABOUT THIS CONTRACT!"

VOIDABLE

A VOIDABLE CONTRACT IS A CONTRACT THAT MAY BE VOIDED IN FULL OR IN PART BY ONE OR BOTH PARTIES. IN MOST CASES, CONTRACTS ARE VOIDABLE BECAUSE ONE OF THE PARTIES WAS A MINOR OR A VICTIM OF FRAUD.

YOU CAN'T ENFORCE THIS CONTRACT AGAINST ME! I'M A MINOR! HA!

WHAT! YOU DIDN'T TELL ME THAT! I'M A VICTIM OF FRAUD!

20

THE VALID CONTRACT

A VALID CONTRACT, BE IT ORAL OR WRITTEN,
MUST CONTAIN THREE SPECIFIC ELEMENTS:
AN **OFFER**, WHICH SPECIFIES THE TERMS OF THE
CONTRACT; THE **CONSIDERATION**, OR "TRADE-OFF,"
TO THE OFFER; AND THE **ACCEPTANCE**.

1. OFFER

I WILL GIVE YOU THE WINNING
TICKET IN THE $40 MILLION LOTTERY.
YOU WANT IT?

2. ACCEPTANCE

$40 MILLION! YES!

3. CONSIDERATION

I CAN GET YOU THAT, AND
ALL I WANT IS YOUR CRUMMY
SOUL.

NO PROBLEM.

OFFER

NO CONTRACT HAS YET BEEN MADE WITHOUT SOMEONE FIRST MAKING AN OFFER. AN OFFER IS A PROMISE THAT ONE PERSON MAKES TO ANOTHER. A VALID OFFER MUST BE CLEAR AND DELIBERATE.

"TAKE MY LAWYER... PLEASE."

A SPECIFIC OFFER IS MADE TO A SPECIFIC PERSON OR PARTY AND CANNOT BE ACCEPTED BY ANYONE. A GENERAL OFFER IS OPEN TO ALL.

I AM WILLING TO DEBATE MY OPPONENT ANYTIME HE WISHES. AND I AM WILLING TO SIT DOWN ANYTIME WITH ANY OF MY CONSTITUENTS...

MOST OFFERS ARE HELD VALID ONLY FOR A SPECIFIC PERIOD OF TIME. THE WITHDRAWAL OF AN OFFER MAY BE MADE AT ANY TIME SO LONG AS IT HAS NOT BEEN ACCEPTED.

WILL YOU MARRY ME?

I... I...

TOO LATE! I'VE CHANGED MY MIND

THE WITHDRAWAL OF AN OFFER TERMINATES THE OFFER, AS DOES THE EXPIRATION OF THE SPECIFIED TIME. DEATH OF A NECESSARY PARTY TO A CONTRACT TERMINATES AN OFFER, AS DOES THE DESTRUCTION OF THE SUBJECT MATTER OF AN OFFER. AND FINALLY, AN OFFER IS CONSIDERED WITHDRAWN, TERMINATED AND NULL AND VOID IF THAT OFFER IS NOT ACCEPTED.

DO NOT DISTURB

NO SOLICITORS

SALESMEN STAY AWAY

WELCOME

ACCEPTANCE

IF THERE IS TO BE A VALID CONTRACT, THEN THERE NOT ONLY MUST BE SOMEONE WHO MAKES AN OFFER, THERE MUST ALSO BE SOMEONE ELSE WHO ACCEPTS THE OFFER. IF AN OFFER IS MADE AND ACCEPTANCE IS GIVEN, THEN A VALID CONTRACT IS IN FORCE.

"BUT WHAT ABOUT THE CONSIDERATIONS?"

BASICALLY, CONSIDERATION IS THE "WHAT-FOR" OF CONTRACTS, SINCE PEOPLE RARELY OFFER TO DO, OR PART WITH, SOMETHING FOR NOTHING, CONSIDERATION BECOMES AN IMPORTANT PART OF THE CONTRACT. WHILE CONSIDERATION GENERALLY HAS A MONETARY VALUE, IT DOESN'T ALWAYS.

24

CONSIDERATION

THE PROPOSAL OF MARRIAGE IS AN OFFER THAT MAY INVOLVE MORE CONSIDERATION THAN FINANCIAL SUPPORT.

USUALLY CONSIDERATION IS SIMPLY PRESUMED TO BE IN ANY CONTRACT. THAT IS, SOMEONE PROMISES SOMETHING IN EXCHANGE FOR SOME OTHER CONSIDERATION. LIKEWISE THOSE WHO ACCEPT AN OFFER DO SO BECAUSE SOME CONSIDERATION COMPELS THEM TO.

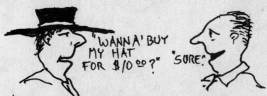

THE ABOVE EXAMPLE HAS ALL THE ELEMENTS OF A BINDING CONTRACT. THE **HAT** IS **OFFERED** FOR A **CONSIDERATION** OF **$ 10.00** AND AN ACCEPTANCE OF THE CONTRACT IS GIVEN.

25

ASSIGNMENTS

WHENEVER TWO PARTIES MAKE A CONTRACT, IT IS GENERALLY UNDERSTOOD THAT THE TERMS OF THE CONTRACT ARE TO BE PERFORMED AND ENFORCED BY THE INTERESTED PARTIES ONLY. HOWEVER, THERE ARE CASES WHERE ONE OR BOTH PARTIES MAY ASSIGN RESPONSIBILITY OF THE CONTRACT TO ANOTHER, THIRD PARTY. ASSIGNMENT DOES NOT RELEASE THE ORIGINAL PARTY (THE ASSIGNOR) FROM RESPONSIBILITY SHOULD THE ASSIGNEE FAIL TO PERFORM THE TERMS OF THE CONTRACT. CONTRACTS THAT REQUIRE THE SPECIAL KNOWLEDGE OR PERSONAL QUALITIES OF ONE OF THE ORIGINAL PARTIES TO THE CONTRACT ARE NOT ASSIGNABLE.

THE INVALID CONTRACT

A CONTRACT IS GOOD ONLY SO FAR AS IT IS ENFORCEABLE IN A COURT OF LAW. AN ILLEGAL CONTRACT (FOR WHATEVER REASON) WILL NOT STAND UP IN COURT. IN SUCH INSTANCES IT IS BEST TO KNOW THE APPLICABLE LAWS OF EACH STATE SINCE THE LAW OF CONTRACT IS A MATTER OF STATE LAW. FOR INSTANCE, SEVERAL STATES HAVE WHAT ARE CALLED "SUNDAY LAWS." THAT IS, A VALID CONTRACT MAY BE NULL AND VOID IF IT WAS ENTERED INTO ON A SUNDAY.

CONTRACTS THAT CANNOT BE PERFORMED BECAUSE OF PROBLEMS BEYOND THE CONTROL OF EITHER PARTY CANNOT BE ENFORCED.

"PLANE CRASH OR NOT, KOWOWSKI, I'VE GOT A CONTRACT HERE SAYS YOU'RE GONNA PLAY BALL!"

-- FRAUD --

FRAUD IS THE DELIBERATE INTENT OF ONE PARTY TO A CONTRACT TO MISLEAD THE OTHER. IF FRAUD IS PROVED, THE MISLED PARTY MAY SUE TO RECOVER FOR LOSSES AND DAMAGES OR THE PARTY MAY SIMPLY END HIS OBLIGATION TO THE TERMS OF THE CONTRACT.

MISREPRESENTATION

MISREPRESENTATION IS NOT FRAUD IN THAT THERE IS NOT THE INTENTION TO MISLEAD. A MIS-REPRESENTED CONTRACT MAY SIMPLY CONTAIN AN INNOCENT ERROR. HOWEVER, IF MISREPRESENTION IS FOUND, EITHER PARTY MAY INVALIDATE THE CONTRACT AND RELIEVE THEMSELVES FROM ANY CONTRACTUAL OBLIGATIONS.

28

DURESS

WHEN A PERSON FEELS HE HAS ENTERED INTO A CONTRACT BECAUSE OF FORCE OR EVEN THE THREAT OF FORCE FROM ANOTHER, HE MAY INVALIDATE THE CONTRACT IN COURT FOR REASONS OF DURESS.

YOU WANNA DO BUSINESS WIT' ME, DON'T YA', PAL?

SURE...

UNDUE INFLUENCE

UNDUE INFLUENCE DOES NOT INVOLVE FORCE OR EVEN THE THREAT OF FORCE. BUT UNDUE INFLUENCE, IF PROVED IN COURT, MAY BE USED IN COURT TO INVALIDATE A CONTRACT. UNDUE INFLUENCE IS THE WRONGFUL INFLUENCE OF ONE PERSON OR PARTY OVER ANOTHER WHO IS IN A WEAKER OR EASILY INFLUENCED POSITION.

"FORGET THE KIDS, NELLY. IT'S YOUR FAITHFUL NURSE SIMS WHO SHOULD OVERSEE YOUR FINANCIAL DEALINGS."

FINE PRINT

THE SUPREME COURT HAS RULED THAT ANY WAIVER OF CONSTITUTIONAL RIGHTS MUST BE "VOLUNTARY," & "INTELLIGENTLY AND KNOWINGLY" MADE, AND THAT THE WAIVER CLAUSE MUST BE CONSPICUOUS IN THE CONTRACT. THIS VIRTUALLY ELIMINATES THE IDEA OF FINE PRINT.

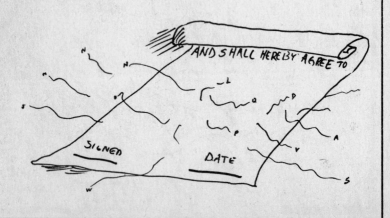

BREACH of CONTRACT

PLANTIFF

DEFENDANT

LIFE IS A BREACH.

ANY NON-PERFORMANCE OF A CONTRACTUAL OBLIGATION IS A BREACH OF CONTRACT. IF ONE PARTY BREACHES A CONTRACT, THE OTHER PARTY MAY SUE TO RECOVER DAMAGES. IN CERTAIN CASES A BREACH OF CONTRACT MAY RESULT IN LOSSES BEYOND THE SCOPE OF THE CONTRACT. IN SUCH CASES IT IS POSSIBLE TO SUE FOR A DECREE OF "SPECIFIC PERFORMANCE."

JACK CAN SUE BOB FOR SPECIFIC PERFORMANCE.
THAT IS, HE CAN RECOVER FROM BOB THE
MONEY HE ADVANCED HIM. OR, JACK CAN SUE
BOB FOR DAMAGES SHOULD BOB TRY TO MARKET
THE INVENTION AS HIS OWN.
FURTHER, JACK HAS THE OPTION OF ASKING
THE COURT FOR AN 'INJUNCTION' WHICH
WOULD MAKE IT ILLEGAL FOR BOB TO DO
ANYTHING WITH THE INVENTION OTHER THAN
WHAT WAS STIPULATED IN THE CONTRACT.

AN EXCEPTION TO THIS IS THE PERSONAL SERVICES
CONTRACT. SPECIFIC PERFORMANCE, IF ENFORCED
BY THE COURT, WOULD, IN EFFECT, AMOUNT TO
PEONAGE OR FORCED LABOR. IN THE EVENT THAT
A PERSONAL SERVICES CONTRACT IS BREACHED,
THE COURT CAN PREVENT THE PERSON FROM
WORKING IN THE SAME CAPACITY FOR ANOTHER
PARTY DURING THE PERIOD OF THE BREACHED CONTRACT.

CONTRACTS & MINORS

A PERSON UNDER THE AGE OF 18 OR 21 (DEPENDING ON THE LAWS OF EACH STATE) IS CONSIDERED A MINOR BY THE COURTS AND AS SUCH IS NOT LEGALLY RESPONSIBLE FOR CONTRACTUAL OBLIGATIONS. FOR THAT REASON FEW PEOPLE ARE WILLING TO FORM AN IMPORTANT CONTRACT WITH A MINOR. EVEN IN A CASE WHERE A MINOR LIES ABOUT HIS AGE IN ORDER TO SECURE A CONTRACT, HE IS STILL NOT LEGALLY BOUND TO FOLLOW THE CONTRACT. FURTHERMORE, A MINOR WHO REACHES THE AGE OF LEGAL MATURITY IS NOT BOUND TO HONOR ANY CONTRACT HE ENTERED INTO AS A MINOR.

HOWEVER, IF A MINOR CAN PROVE THAT HE IS FINANCIALLY INDEPENDENT OF HIS PARENTS, OR IF HE IS MARRIED, OR A MEMBER OF THE ARMED FORCES, HE MAY SEEK A LEGAL RELEASE FROM PARENTAL CUSTODY. HE IS THEN CONSIDERED AN EMANCIPATED MINOR AND LEGALLY ABLE TO ENTER INTO AND BE HELD RESPONSIBLE FOR CONTRACTS.

33

CASE STUDY

MR. CURDLE HIRES MS. BULK TO COME TO HIS HOME AND PREPARE A GOURMET MEAL FOR HIMSELF AND HIS IMPORTANT GUESTS....

"I'LL PAY YOU FIVE HUNDRED DOLLARS TO PREPARE ONE OF YOUR FAMOUS MEALS."

"O.K."

THAT AFTERNOON MS. BULK LEARNS SHE HAS A ONCE-IN-A-LIFETIME OPPORTUNITY TO COOK FOR HANDSOME TV STAR VAN GRIT.

"VAN GRIT WANTS TO EAT MY GOULASH!"

MS. BULK ASSIGNS HER VERBAL CONTRACT WITH MR. CURDLE TO VONA SHEEF, HER ABLE ASSISTANT. THAT EVENING, VONA'S ARRIVAL AT MR. CURDLE'S HOME IS GREETED WITH DISMAY.

WHERE IS MS. BULK?"

"AN ACT OF GOD PREVENTED HER PRESENCE HERE TONIGHT."

"BUT I... THIS IS BAD... MY GUESTS WILL SOON BE HERE."

CURSING GOD AND HIS UNTIMELY ACTS, MR. CURDLE ACCEPTS VONA SHEEF'S OFFER TO COOK IN MS. BULK'S ABSENCE. THE DINNER PARTY IS A SUCCESS.

"A SCRUMPTUOUS FEAST, I MUST SAY."

"THANK YOU, THANK YOU."

"GREAT DIGS, POP."

UPON RETIRING THAT NIGHT, MR. CURDLE IS SHOCKED TO SEE A BEAMING MS. BULK SERVING FOOD TO HANDSOME TV STAR VAN GRIT ON THE LATE NIGHT NEWS.

"HEY!"

"YOM, GOOO!"

"OOOOOOOOOOH!"

THE NEXT DAY MR. CURDLE SUES MS. BULK FOR BREACH OF CONTRACT.

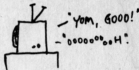

MMM GOOD!

"YOUR HONOR, I HAD A SPECIFIC PERFORMANCE CONTRACT WITH MS. BULK. SHE INTENTION- ALLY BREACHED. I SEEK DAMAGES."

MR. CURDLE CLAIMED THAT HIS CONTRACT WITH VONA WAS MADE UNDER DURESS (HE HAD NO CHOICE, HIS GUESTS WERE ARRIVING SOON) AND THEREFORE VOID. THE COURT DISAGREED. VONA'S FOOD WAS PER MS. BULK'S PRECISE INSTRUCTIONS. THE MOST IMPORTANT CONSIDERATION OF HIS CON- TRACT WITH MS. BULK WAS HER FOOD, NOT HER PRESENCE.

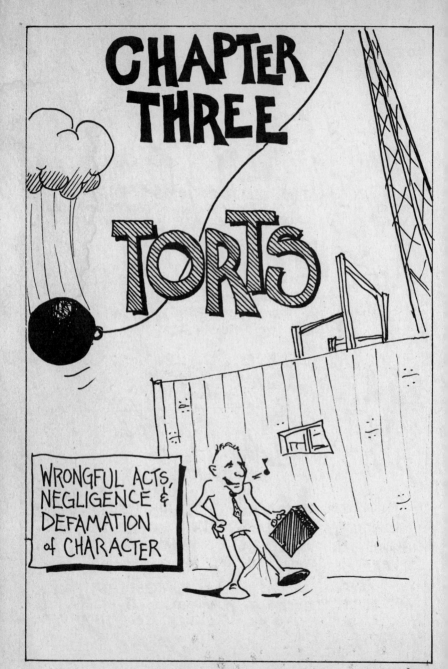

EVERYONE HAS HEARD OF CIVIL RIGHTS
(AND IN THE NEXT CHAPTER WE'LL LOOK
AT CIVIL RIGHTS AND THE LAW), BUT WHAT
ABOUT CIVIL WRONGS? WHEN WE VIOLATE
SOMEONE'S CIVIL RIGHTS WE COMMIT A
CIVIL WRONG, OR WHAT THE LAW CALLS
A TORT.

WRONGFUL ACT | NEGLIGENCE | DEFAMATION of CHARACTER

TORTS, OR CIVIL WRONGS, GENERALLY COME
IN ONE OF THREE WAYS: (1) THROUGH AN IN-
TENTIONAL WRONGFUL ACT THAT HARMS BODY AND/OR
PROPERTY, INCLUDING ASSAULT, BATTERY, TRESPASS
AND OTHER NASTY THINGS; (2) THROUGH NEGLIGENCE,
WHICH UNINTENTIONALLY BRINGS ABOUT AN
UNHAPPY END; AND (3) THROUGH DEFAMATION OF
CHARACTER, WHICH HARMS A PERSON'S REP-
UTATION.

THE WRONGFUL ACT

THIS IS THE INTENTIONAL ACT OF MESSING WITH ANOTHER'S PERSON OR PROPERTY.

ASSAULT

ASSAULT DOES NOT INVOLVE PHYSICAL CONTACT WITH ANOTHER PERSON. ASSAULT IS ONLY THE IMMEDIATE THREAT OF PHYSICAL CONTACT.

BATTERY

by WHAM

IF ASSAULT IS THE BARK, BATTERY IS THE BITE. BATTERY IS ANY INTENTIONAL, OFFENSIVE CONTACT WITH ANOTHER PERSON. THE COURTS INTERPRET THIS AS ANY UNWELCOME PHYSICAL CONTACT, EVEN IF THERE WAS NO INTENT TO HARM AND NO HOSTILITY INVOLVED.

AM I LIABLE IF?....
"...IF I ASSAULT AND BATTER A GUY IN SELF-DEFENSE?"
A
B
MAYBE. EVERY INDIVIDUAL HAS THE RIGHT TO DEFEND HIMSELF, HIS PROPERTY AND HIS FAMILY. HOWEVER, SELF-DEFENSE IS PERMISSIBLE ONLY SO FAR AS NEEDED TO RESIST AN ATTACK. GETTING THE UPPER HAND ON AN ATTACKER, THEN PUMMELING HIM MAY MAKE ONE LIABLE FOR DAMAGES.
...IF MY PET BITES SOMEONE?
WELL, MOST PETS GET WHAT MIGHT BE CONSIDERED ONE FIRST BITE. AFTER THAT THEY'RE CONSIDERED MEAN, AND THE PET OWNER WILL PROBABLY BE LIABLE.
...IF I HIRE SOME GUY TO DRIVE A TRUCK AND THIS GUY DECIDES TO SHORTCUT THROUGH A PLAYGROUND?
UNDER THE RULE "RESPONDEAT SUPERIOR,"* AN EMPLOYER IS RESPONSIBLE FOR THE ACTS OF HIS EMPLOYEES DURING THE COURSE OF THEIR JOB-RELATED ACTIVITIES.
* OR "LET THE BOSS RESPOND TO THE CLAIM."

FALSE ARREST

EVERY PERSON HAS THE RIGHT TO PERSONAL LIBERTY. WHEN A PERSON IS ARRESTED, THERE MUST BE A WARRANT FOR HIS ARREST OR THE ARRESTING OFFICER MUST HAVE A VALID REASON FOR MAKING AN ARREST. A PRIVATE CITIZEN MAY ARREST ANOTHER IF HE HAS WITNESSED A CRIME. OTHERWISE, HE MAY BE LIABLE FOR FALSE ARREST.

WHAT DID I DO?

YOU JUST LOOK LIKE TROUBLE.

FALSE IMPRISONMENT

IN THE CASE OF FALSE ARREST IT IS ASSUMED THAT BY ARRESTING SOMEONE UNLAWFULLY YOU'RE DETAINING HIM UNLAWFULLY AS WELL. THERE-FORE, FALSE IMPRISONMENT IS THE UNLAWFUL DETENTION OF ANOTHER WITHOUT JUSTIFICATION, AND AGAINST HIS WILL.

LET ME GO! YOU CANT DO THIS!

EMOTIONAL DISTRESS

GENERALLY SPEAKING, PEOPLE ARE NOT LIABLE
FOR INFLICTING EMOTIONAL DISTRESS ON
OTHERS UNLESS IT IS ACCOMPANIED BY ACTUAL
PHYSICAL INJURY OR THEIR DISTRESS IS THE
DIRECT RESULT OF AN ILLEGAL ACT.

TRESPASS

TRESPASS IS THE VIOLATION OF ANOTHER'S PROPERTY RIGHTS. THIS CAN MEAN A VARIETY OF TORTS BEYOND SIMPLY WALKING ACROSS SOMEONE'S BACKYARD.

A. IF A BUILDING'S OVERHANG WERE TO EXTEND OVER ANOTHER'S PROPERTY LINE, A TRESPASS WOULD OCCUR.

B. TRESSPASS OCCURS WHEN SOMEONE THROWS OR PLACES ANY UNWANTED ITEM ONTO ANOTHER'S PROPERTY.

C. DIGGING, EVEN IF DONE LEGALLY, ON ONE'S OWN LAND, CAN BE CONSIDERED TRESPASSING IF IT IN ANY WAY ALTERS THE LAND OR AFFECTS THE BUILDINGS OF ANOTHER.

NUISANCE

NUISANCE IS SORT OF THE FLIP SIDE OF THE TRESPASS COIN. THAT IS, WHEN A PERSON USES HIS PROPERTY IN A WAY THAT IS OBJECTIONABLE TO HIS NEIGHBORS, HE MAY BE COMMITTING THE TORT OF NUISANCE.

TYPES of NUISANCE

OBJECTIONABLE ODOR

HANGOUT FOR UN-SAVORY CHARACTERS.

OBJECTIONABLY LOUD NOISE.

OH WOW! AN OLD REFRIGERATOR!

STAY OUT PRIVATE PROPERTY

AN EXISTING DANGEROUS CONDITION, EVEN ON PRIVATE PROPERTY, MAY CONSTITUTE A NUISANCE IF IT ATTRACTS AND IS POTENTIALLY DANGEROUS.

CONVERSION

WHILE TRESPASS PERTAINS TO REAL PROPERTY, CONVERSION IS A TORT PERTAINING TO ALL OTHER PERSONAL PROPERTY. IN MANY CASES, CONVERSION IS AN OPEN, USUALLY INNOCENT ACT.

DARN! THIS THING WON'T START... SAY, BILL'S ON VACATION... MAYBE I'LL JUST WALK OVER AND BORROW HIS MOWER.

GEESH! WHAT A CRIME-INFESTED NEIGHBORHOOD!

THE ABOVE ACTION WOULD BE CONVERSION, SINCE CONVERSION IS EITHER USING ANOTHER'S PROPERTY WITHOUT THEIR KNOWLEDGE, OR USING THEIR PROPERTY WITH APPROVAL BUT THEN USING IT IN SOME UN-ACCEPTABLE MANNER. PERHAPS THE MOST LITIGATED FORM OF CONVERSION IS WHEN ONE PERSON SELLS PROPERTY BELONGING TO ANOTHER.

YOU DID WHAT?!?

YEA... FOR THE SUMMER!

OH, I UH SOLD YOUR MOWER... YOU SAID I COULD HAVE IT...

OH... I GUESS I THOUGHT YOU MEANT I COULD HAVE IT...

44

NEGLIGENCE

WHOOPS!

NEGLIGENCE IS CONSIDERED A CARELESS OR RECKLESS ACT. IT IS **NOT** AN INTENTIONAL HARM. NEGLIGENCE IS ALSO DEFINED AS THE FAILURE TO USE REASONABLE CARE IN THE PERFORMANCE OF SOME DUTY. THE RESULT OF NEGLIGENCE IS ALMOST ALWAYS AN ACCIDENT. DETERMINING WHO WAS "AT FAULT" WHEN AN ACCIDENT OCCURS, AND TO WHAT DEGREE, IS THE JOB OF THE COURT. THE LIABILITY FOR NEGLIGENCE VARIES GREATLY FROM STATE TO STATE BECAUSE EVERY STATE DETERMINES NEGLIGENCE DIFFERENTLY.

NEGLIGENCE

CONTRIBUTORY

WHEN ONE PERSON'S NEGLIGENCE CAUSES AN ACCIDENT, IT'S EASY TO DETERMINE RESPONSIBILITY. BUT HOW ARE NEGLIGENCE AND LIABILITY DETERMINED WHEN MORE THAN ONE PERSON IS NEGLIGENT? FOR STATES THAT ABIDE BY THE NOTION OF CONTRIBUTORY NEGLIGENCE, NEITHER PARTY TO AN ACCIDENT CAN MAKE A CLAIM AGAINST THE OTHER IF BOTH PARTIES (EVEN SLIGHTLY SO) CONTRIBUTED NEGLIGENCE.

VS

MOST STATES PREFER THE IDEA OF COMPARATIVE NEGLIGENCE. THAT IS, WHEN AN ACCIDENT OCCURS AND BOTH PARTIES SHARE RESPONSIBILITY, THE COURTS WILL SEEK TO DETERMINE TO WHAT EXTENT (HENCE, WHAT LIABILITY) EACH PARTY IS TO BLAME FOR THE ACCIDENT.
FOR EXAMPLE, IF MR. B HAS A $10,000.00 CLAIM AGAINST MR. A, BUT MR. B IS 25% RESPONSIBLE FOR CAUSING THE ACCIDENT, THEN MR. A IS ONLY LIABLE TO MR. B FOR $7,500.00.

COMPARATIVE

LAST CLEAR CHANCE

SOMETIMES PEOPLE CARELESSLY EXPOSE THEM-SELVES AND OTHERS TO DANGER. WHEN AN ACCIDENT RESULTS, THEIR CARELESSNESS USUALLY MAKES THEM LIABLE, BUT NOT ALWAYS. ACCORDING TO THE DOCTRINE OF LAST CLEAR CHANCE, A CARELESS PARTY MAY NOT BE FULLY LIABLE IF THE OTHER PARTY (EVEN WITH THE RIGHT OF WAY) HAD SOME CHANCE TO AVOID THE ACCIDENT.

WOW, LOOK WAYNE! PEDESTRIANS CROSSING AGAINST THE LIGHT! FLOOR IT, BUDDY, SCORE SOME POINTS!

FORGET IT, SID. I MAY HAVE THE RIGHT OF WAY, BUT THE LAW STATES THAT IF I CAN AVOID AN ACCIDENT, BUT DON'T, I AM LIABLE TOO.

DOES THIS GUY KNOW THE MEAN-ING OF FUN, OR WHAT?

DEFAMATION OF CHARACTER

DEFAMATION OF CHARACTER COMES IN TWO SIZES: SMALL & LARGE.

SLANDER

YOU WANT TO KNOW WHAT'S WRONG WITH JACK? THE GUY'S AN ALCHOHOLIC. HE DRINKS BECAUSE HE'S INCOMPETENT... SEE, THE GUY WAS THROWN OUT OF HIGH SCHOOL ... FOR HITTING A NUN!

SLANDER IS ORAL DEFAMATION. IT IS A FALSE ACCUSATION THAT IS MEANT TO HARM THE REPUTATION OF ANOTHER.

LIBEL

...IN SHORT, THE MAN IS A CROOK AND A MENACE TO DECENT SOCIETY...

LIBEL IS BIG-TIME SLANDER. THAT IS, SLANDER BECOMES LIBEL WHEN IT IS "PUBLISHED" OR BROADCAST FOR ALL, OR EVEN JUST ONE, TO SEE. BOTH LIBEL AND SLANDER ARE ACTIONABLE AS TORTS, EVEN IF NO SPECIAL HARM RESULTS. A SLANDEROUS COMMENT CAN GET A PERSON IN A LOT OF TROUBLE. BUT THERE ARE SOME DEFENSES AVAILABLE TO A PERSON ACCUSED OF DEFAMATION.

DEFENSES
1. THE TRUTH

LET'S FACE IT, IF SOMEONE LIFTS YOUR WALLET YOU CAN CALL HIM A THIEF WITHOUT FEAR OF PROSECUTION. BUT CALL HIM SOMETHING HE'S NOT AND YOU MAY BE LIABLE.

2. CONSENT

IF YOU WANT TO SLANDER OR LIBEL SOMEONE AND BE FREE FROM TORT, SIMPLY GET THEIR CONSENT FIRST.

3. PRIVILEGE

AS IF THEY DIDN'T ALREADY HAVE ENOUGH PRIVILEGES, JUDGES AND LAWYERS ARE IMMUNE FROM LIABILITY FOR MAKING DEFAMATORY STATEMENTS DURING THE COURSE OF DOING THEIR JOB IN THE COURTROOM.

4. FAIR COMMENT

IF YOU'RE A PUBLIC FIGURE, THEN PEOPLE ARE ALLOWED TO SLANDER AND LIBEL YOU SO LONG AS THEIR REMARKS ARE CONSTRUED AS FAIR AND REASONABLE OR HONEST OPINIONS CONCERNING THE SUBJECT'S PUBLIC LIFE.

5. HUSBAND & WIFE IN SOME STATES

SPOUSES CAN WALK AROUND THE HOUSE ALL DAY AND SLANDER ANYONE TO EACH OTHER, SINCE COMMON LAW HOLDS THAT MAN & WIFE ARE ONE PERSON.

CASE STUDY

HOWIE AGREES TO RENT HIS BOAT TO BENNETT SO THAT BENNETT CAN FISH FOR BASS ON LAKE OBLONG.

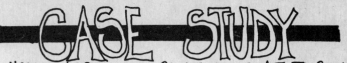

ON THE OTHER SIDE OF LAKE OBLONG, BENNETT ENCOUNTERS MR. & MRS. WAKE CHUBB. THE CHUBBS OFFER TO PAY BENNETT TO GIVE THEM A BOAT RIDE AROUND THE LAKE. AS IT'S SLOW FISHING, BENNETT ACCEPTS.

UNFORTUNATELY, A PATCH ON THE BOAT GIVES WAY. WITHIN MOMENTS THE BOAT SINKS.

BACK ON SHORE   BENNETT CLAIMS THAT THE BOAT SANK BECAUSE OF A FAULTY PATCHING JOB AND THEREFORE HOWIE IS TO BE HELD LIABLE FOR NEGLIGENCE. BENNETT THEN CHARGES MR. CHUBB WITH SLANDER BY CALLING HIM A LOUSY SKIPPER, WHEN IN FACT HE WAS NO SKIPPER AT ALL, JUST A FISHERMAN.

"I'M CALLING MY LAWYER... YOU GUYS ARE IN ALOT OF TROUBLE."

MUCH TO BENNETT'S DISMAY IT WAS HE WHO WAS IN A LOT OF TROUBLE. BENNETT HAD COMMITTED THE CRIME OF CONVERSION WHEN HE ALTERED HIS AGREED-TO USE OF HOWIE'S FISHING BOAT TO AN UNACCEPTABLE USE AS A PLEASURE SPEED BOAT. THIS MEANT THAT BENNETT WAS HELD RESPONSIBLE NOT ONLY FOR THE ACCIDENT BUT ALSO FOR THE LOSS OF THE BOAT. AS FOR BENNETT'S CHARGE THAT MR. CHUBB HAD SLANDERED HIM, AGAIN HE WAS ALL WET. EVEN THOUGH BENNETT MAY HAVE INITIALLY PRESENTED HIMSELF AS A FISHERMAN, WHEN HE AGREED TO PILOT MR. & MRS. CHUBB HE "PUT ON A SAILOR'S CAP." AND AS SUCH, MR. CHUBB WAS FULLY JUSTIFIED IN OFFERING AN HONEST ASSESSMENT OF MR. BENNETT'S NAUTICAL SKILLS.

CHAPTER FOUR

CIVIL RIGHTS

FREEDOM of EXPRESSION,
RELIGION AND ASSEMBLY

THE FIRST AMENDMENT TO THE CONSTITUTION STATES:

"CONGRESS SHALL MAKE NO LAW RESPECTING AN ESTABLISHMENT OF RELIGION, OR PROHIBITING THE FREE EXERCISE THEREOF; OR ABRIDGING THE FREEDOM OF SPEECH, OR OF THE PRESS; OR THE RIGHT OF THE PEOPLE PEACEABLY TO ASSEMBLE, AND TO PETITION THE GOVERNMENT FOR A REDRESS OF GRIEVANCES."

THE CONSTITUTION IS THE DOCUMENT THAT GUARANTEES THE BASIC RIGHTS OF CITIZENS. CONSTITUTIONAL LAW CONCERNS THE PROTECTION OF THESE RIGHTS, KNOWN ALSO AS CIVIL RIGHTS.

ONE ORGANIZATION THAT WORKS HARD TO PROTECT THE CONSTITUTIONAL RIGHTS OF ALL CITIZENS IS THE AMERICAN CIVIL LIBERTIES UNION (A.C.L.U.)

RELIGIOUS FREEDOM

THE CONSTITUTION GUARANTEES THAT THERE WILL BE NO STATE-SPONSORED OR STATE-SUPPORTED CHURCH.

THE CONSTITUTION ALSO GUARANTEES THAT EVERYONE CAN WORSHIP THEIR GOD AS THEY SEE FIT, WITHOUT FEAR OF PERSECUTION, SO LONG AS THEIR RELIGIOUS PRACTICES ARE NOT COUNTER TO THE LAWS OF THE STATE.

56

FREEDOM of THOUGHT

WHILE THERE ARE RESTRICTIONS TO FREE EX-
PRESSION, FREE THOUGHT IS SACRED. FREEDOM
OF THOUGHT DOES NOT JUST MEAN THAT
PEOPLE ARE FREE TO THINK ANYTHING THEY
CHOOSE (WHICH WOULD BE DIFFICULT FOR GOVERN-
MENT TO CONTROL)...

...FREEDOM OF THOUGHT ALSO MEANS THAT
THE GOVERNMENT CANNOT MANDATE OR PENAL-
IZE ANYONE FOR THINKING OR NOT THINKING IN
ANY PARTICULAR WAY.

"YOU WANT YOUR SOCIAL SECURITY? THEN SIGN
THE STATEMENT SAYING YOU THINK YOUR GOVERNMENT
IS DOING A GOOD JOB."

FREEDOM of ASSEMBLY

THE CONSTITUTION GUARANTEES THAT PEOPLE HAVE THE RIGHT TO GET TOGETHER IN PUBLIC PLACES AND EVEN TAKE THEMSELVES SERIOUSLY. THE CONSTITUTION ALSO SAYS PEOPLE HAVE THE RIGHT TO ASSOCIATE WITH ANYONE, NO MATTER HOW SILLY THAT PERSON MAY BE.

BEEP BEEP!

"DON'T YOU GUYS SEE WHAT HE'S SAYING... HE'S SAYING THAT OUR TAX STRUCTURE BENEFITS THE RICH..."

"ONE MORE ON THE LIGHTER SIDE"

FREEDOM to ASSEMBLE EXPRESSIONS

ONE RARELY MENTIONED FREEDOM WE AMERICANS HAVE IS THE RIGHT TO ASSEMBLE EXPRESSIONS.

"YOU CAN LEAD A HORSE TO WATER BUT YOU CAN'T MAKE HIM TOUCH BASE WITH A NICE DAY."

"AN APPLE SAVED IS A PENNY TO A BLIND MAN."

PERSONAL FREEDOMS

ONE OF THE MOST VIGOROUSLY PROTECTED FREEDOMS IN THE UNITED STATES IS THE RIGHT TO BEAR ARMS.

EVEN THOUGH ALL CITIZENS HAVE THE RIGHT TO OWN GUNS, SEVERAL STATES AND COMMUNITIES PLACE TIGHT CONTROLS ON SALES OF GUNS AND REQUIRE LICENSES FOR THOSE WHO WISH TO OWN THEM.

WOMEN'S RIGHTS

AS OF NOW, WOMEN ENJOY ALL THE BASIC CONSTITUTIONAL RIGHTS GUARANTEED TO ALL CITIZENS. THIS IS ASSURED BY THE 14TH AMENDMENT, WHICH SAYS THAT NO STATE SHALL ABRIDGE THE RIGHTS OF ITS CITIZENS ACCORDED TO THEM BY THE CONSTITUTION, **AND**, THE 19TH AMENDMENT, WHICH SPECIFICALLY STATES THAT NO CITIZENS CAN BE DENIED THEIR RIGHTS ON THE BASIS OF SEX. AS FOR THE PROPOSED EQUAL RIGHTS AMENDMENT (E.R.A.), WHICH SIMPLY STATES THAT EQUAL PROTECTION CANNOT BE DENIED ON THE BASIS OF SEX, ITS EFFECT WOULD DEPEND UPON ITS INTERPRETATION BY THE COURTS. FURTHER, THE POWER TO ENFORCE THE PROTECTION ACCORDED WOMEN BY THE E.R.A WOULD SHIFT FROM THE INDIVIDUAL STATES TO THE FEDERAL GOVERNMENT. SUGGESTING, IN PART, WHY SOME STATES ARE RELUCTANT TO RATIFY THE E.R.A.

THE CONSTITUTION GUARANTEES ALL CITIZENS THE RIGHT TO PRIVACY. FOR WOMEN, THIS MEANS A RIGHT TO CONTROL THEIR BODIES, OR IN OTHER WORDS, THEIR RIGHT TO HAVE AN ABORTION. BUT THIS MAY CHANGE. ALREADY STATES HAVE THE RIGHT TO REGULATE ABORTIONS AFTER THE FIRST THREE MONTHS OF PREGNANCY, AND AFTER SIX MONTHS THE STATE MAY FORBID THE ABORTION.

DO NOT OPEN STATE ORDER

THE CONSTITUTION ALSO PROTECTS WOMEN FROM JOB DISCRIMINATION, AND CONSUMER CREDIT LAWS MAKE IT ILLEGAL FOR CREDITORS TO REFUSE CREDIT ON THE BASIS OF SEX.

RIGHTS of the ACCUSED

AN ARRESTED PERSON HAS THE RIGHT TO KNOW WHAT CRIME HE IS BEING ARRESTED FOR.

"...THE RIGHT TO REMAIN SILENT. ANYTHING YOU SAY CAN AND WILL BE USED AGAINST YOU AND MAY BE INCLUDED IN MY BOOK WITHOUT YOUR CONSENT. IF THIS IS NOT AMIABLE TO YOU, YOU HAVE THE RIGHT TO CONTACT AN AGENT..."

- MIRANDA -

IN THE MIRANDA CASE, THE SUPREME COURT RULED THAT ALL PERSONS PLACED UNDER ARREST MUST BE ADVISED OF THEIR CONSTITUTIONAL RIGHTS. ESSENTIALLY, THESE ARE THE RIGHT TO REMAIN SILENT AND THE 'RIGHT TO HAVE AN ATTORNEY PRESENT DURING QUESTIONING. "MIRANDA" ALSO STATES THAT THE COURTS MUST PROVIDE AN ATTORNEY IF THE ACCUSED CANNOT AFFORD ONE.

IN ADDITION TO MIRANDA, THE ACCUSED ALSO HAVE THE RIGHT TO BE RELEASED FROM JAIL UNTIL THEIR TRIAL (WITH SOME EXCEPTIONS) ON THEIR OWN RECOGNIZANCE (GOOD REPUTATION) OR, BY POSTING BAIL (MONEY WHICH WOULD BE FORFEITED IF THE ACCUSED DID NOT APPEAR FOR TRIAL). FINALLY, THE ACCUSED HAS THE RIGHT TO BE JUDGED BY A JURY OF HIS PEERS AND THE RIGHT TO FACE HIS ACCUSER IN OPEN COURT.

VICTIM'S RIGHTS

WHILE THE CONSTITUTION DOES NOT OFFER ANY SPECIFIC RIGHTS FOR VICTIMS OF CRIME, STATE LEGISLATURES HAVE BEEN WRITING NEW LAWS OR ENFORCING OLD ONES THAT PROVIDE COMPENSATION FOR VICTIMS OF CRIMES AND PROTECTION FOR WITNESSES TO CRIMES. VICTIM COMPENSATION PROGRAMS ALREADY EXIST IN MANY STATES, AND LATELY, VICTIMS AND/OR THEIR FAMILIES HAVE BEEN ABLE TO RECOVER FROM ANY BOOK AND/OR MOVIE SALES THAT ARE BASED ON THE EXPLOITS OF A CRIMINAL.

CONSTITUTIONAL AMENDMENTS

— A REVIEW —

1. THE FIRST AMENDMENT IS A CATCHALL THAT GUARANTEES THE FREEDOM OF RELIGION, FREEDOM OF THE PRESS AND THE FREEDOM TO PEACEABLY ASSEMBLE.

2. THE SECOND AMENDMENT GUARANTEES THE RIGHT OF CITIZENS TO BEAR ARMS.

3. THE THIRD AMENDMENT STATES THAT THE GOVERNMENT CANNOT HOUSE SOLDIERS IN PRIVATE HOMES DURING TIMES OF PEACE.

4. THE FORTH AMENDMENT PROTECTS WITNESSES FROM SELF-INCRIMINATION.

5. THE FIFTH AMENDMENT IS ANOTHER CATCHALL.

A. A PERSON ACCUSED OF A CAPITAL CRIME MUST BE FIRST INDICTED BY A GRAND JURY.

B. THE FIFTH AMENDMENT FORBIDS SOMETHING CALLED "DOUBLE JEOPARDY" THAT IS, THE POSSIBILITY OF SOMEONE'S BEING TRIED TWICE FOR THE SAME CRIME.

C. THIS IS A FAVORITE PROVISION WITH MOBSTERS. IT PROTECTS WITNESSES FROM TESTIFYING AGAINST THEMSELVES IN A CRIMINAL PROSECUTION.

5. CONTINUED

D. THIS GUARANTEES THAT NO PERSON SHALL BE DEPRIVED OF DUE PROCESS OF LAW. THAT IS, GUARANTEEING ACCUSED OF ANY CRIME HIS FULL BENEFIT FROM THE PROCESS OF THE LEGAL JUSTICE SYSTEM.

E. THIS PROVIDES THAT PRIVATE PROPERTY SHALL NOT BE MADE PUBLIC WITHOUT FAIR COMPENSATION FOR THE OWNER.

6. THE SIXTH AMENDMENT GAURANTEES THE RIGHTS OF THE ACCUSED. THAT IS, THEIR RIGHT TO A SPEEDY TRIAL, A TRIAL BY A JURY OF THEIR PEERS AND THE RIGHT TO HAVE AN ATTORNEY PRESENT IN THEIR BEHALF.

8. THE EIGHTH AMENDMENT FORBIDS CRUEL AND UNUSUAL PUNISHMENT OR THE SETTING OF EXCESSIVELY HIGH BAIL OR FINES.

13. THE THIRTEENTH AMENDMENT ABOLISHES SLAVERY AND OTHER FORMS OF FORCED LABOR.

14. A SORT OF FEDERAL GUARANTEE THAT NO **STATE** SHALL ABRIDGE OR DENY RIGHTS GUARANTEED BY THE CONSTITUTION.

15. THE FIFTEENTH AMENDMENT IS THE VOTING RIGHTS AMENDMENT. THIS IS MEANT TO ENSURE THAT ALL CITIZENS HAVE EQUAL RIGHTS TO VOTE.

19. WHEREAS PRIOR AMENDMENTS SPECIFY THAT RIGHTS CANNOT BE DENIED BY REASONS OF RACE, CREED OR RELIGION, THE NINETEENTH AMENDMENT EXTENDS THE WORDING TO INCLUDE SEX.

CHAPTER FIVE

CONSUMER PROTECTION

CAVEAT EMPTOR

- OR -

"LET THE BUYER BEWARE"

UNTIL VERY RECENTLY, CONSUMER PROTECTION WAS LITTLE MORE THAN "CAVEAT EMPTOR." THAT MAY HAVE BEEN FINE IN THE DAYS WHEN MANUFACTURERS WERE SMALL AND GEOGRAPHICALLY LIMITED AND WORD OF MOUTH COULD POSSIBLY PUT A BAD MANUFACTURER OUT OF BUSINESS, BUT TODAY WITH MASS MANUFACTURING AND GLOBAL MARKETING, SHODDY PRODUCTS CAN CONTINUE TO BE SOLD WITH LITTLE ADVERSE EFFECT FROM WORD OF MOUTH. SINCE THIS MEANT A PROFUSION OF LOW-QUALITY, OFTEN UNSAFE, PRODUCTS, GOVERNMENT HAD TO STEP IN TO PROTECT THE CONSUMER.

THE FEDERAL CONSUMER PRODUCT SAFETY ACT

ENACTED BY CONGRESS, AND OVERSEEN BY THE FEDERAL CONSUMER PRODUCT SAFETY COMMISSION, THIS ACT GAVE THE COMMISSION THE AUTHORITY TO ESTABLISH SAFETY STANDARDS FOR CONSUMER PRODUCTS AND THE AUTHORITY TO ENFORCE THOSE STANDARDS.

THE MAGNUSON-MOSS FEDERAL TRADE COMMISSION IMPROVEMENT ACT

BESIDES BEING A MOUTHFUL, THIS ACT HELPS TO CLARIFY THE KIND OF WARRANTY A PRODUCT HAS, BE IT A FULL OR LIMITED WARRANTY. A FULL WARRANTY MEANS THAT THE CONSUMER HAS THE RIGHT TO A FULL REFUND OR REPLACEMENT.

69

UNFAIR & DECEPTIVE
➤ PRACTICES ◄

SINCE MANY OF THE UNFAIR, DECEPTIVE
AND FRAUDULENT PRACTICES ARE SOLICITED TO
CONSUMERS THROUGH THE MAIL, THE U.S. POSTAL
SERVICE HAS ESTABLISHED ITS OWN CONSUMER
PROTECTION DEPARTMENT WHICH WARNS CON-
SUMERS WHAT TO BE WARY OF AND PURSUES
CONSUMER COMPLAINTS. ALSO, MOST STATES
HAVE ENACTED LAWS THAT ARE ALSO DE-
SIGNED TO PROTECT CONSUMERS FROM
MAIL FRAUD

① " WOW, THIS AD SAYS I CAN HAVE A FULL HEAD OF HAIR IN JUST 4-6 WEEKS, IF I SEND JUST $50.00 THROUGH THE MAIL FOR THEIR PRODUCT."

② "JUST IMAGINE, ME WITH A FULL HEAD OF HAIR!"

③ SIX WEEKS LATER

"SIGN HERE."

④ "HEY! THIS ISN'T THE FULL HEAD OF HAIR I HAD IN MIND."

DOOR-TO-DOOR SALES

MOST STATES HAVE ENACTED RESTRICTIONS ON DOOR-TO-DOOR SALES. THIS HAS NOTHING TO DO WITH ONE DOOR SELLING TO ANOTHER DOOR, BUT RATHER, IT REFERS TO HIGH-PRESSURE SALESMEN WHO PREY ON FOLKS AT HOME. TO PROTECT UNWARY CONSUMERS FROM BEING PRESSURED INTO BUYING A PRODUCT THEY DON'T REALLY WANT, MOST STATES HAVE ENACTED A FORM OF LEGISLATION COMMONLY REFERED TO AS "COOLING-OFF PERIOD." THIS ALLOWS A CONSUMER TO RETURN A DOWN PAYMENT OR A PRODUCT FOR A FULL REFUND WITHIN A TWO-DAY OR THREE-DAY WAITING PERIOD.

FALSE ADVERTISING

MOST STATES PROHIBIT FALSE ADVERTISING. THE MOST COMMON FORM OF FALSE, OR MISLEADING, ADVERTISING IS CALLED BAIT AND SWITCH.

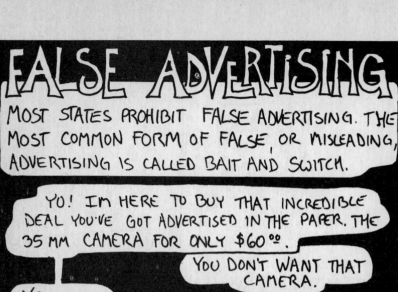

YO! I'M HERE TO BUY THAT INCREDIBLE DEAL YOU'VE GOT ADVERTISED IN THE PAPER. THE 35 MM CAMERA FOR ONLY $60.00.

YOU DON'T WANT THAT CAMERA.

YES I DO.

LOOK, I COULD SELL YOU THAT CAMERA BUT YOU'D HATE ME FOR IT. I'VE GOT A MUCH BETTER CAMERA FOR ONLY $30.00 MORE.

BUT I WANT THE ONE YOU ADVERTISED.

FORGET THAT. FOR ONLY ANOTHER $50.00 I CAN GET YOU A REALLY GREAT CAMERA...

BUT I...

YOU DON'T WANT TO THROW AWAY YOUR $60.00 BUCKS WHEN YOU CAN PUT THAT MONEY DOWN ON A REAL DEAL.

HMM, WELL MAYBE...

CONSUMER CREDIT

IN 1968 CONGRESS PASSED THE CONSUMER CREDIT PROTECTION ACT. AMONG THE VARIOUS REFORMS ENACTED WERE:

TRUTH IN LENDING
A.K.A.
REGULATION Z

REGULATION Z REQUIRES CREDITORS TO SPELL OUT THE CREDIT ARRANGEMENTS BEING MADE TO A CONSUMER WHO WISHES TO MAKE A PURCHASE ON CREDIT.

WILL THIS BE CASH OR CHARGE?

I'D LIKE TO CHARGE IT, IF IT'S NO PROBLEM...

NO MA'AM. WE OFFER A ROTATING ACCOUNT THAT HAS A SIMPLE 18% FINANCE CHARGE ON A CLOSED-END TWELVE-MONTH TERM OR YOU CAN APPLY FOR A HOUSEMAKER LOAN...

THE CREDIT·CARD

"HEY HOLD ON... WAIT FOR ME....!"

ACCORDING TO THE PROVISIONS OF THE ACT, A CREDITOR CANNOT ISSUE A CREDIT CARD TO A CONSUMER UNLESS THAT PERSON APPLIES FOR IT. IF A CONSUMER RECEIVES A CREDIT CARD THAT HE HAS NOT REQUESTED, THEN THAT PERSON IS NOT LIABLE FOR ANY UNAUTHORIZED USE OF THE CARD. HOWEVER, IF THE PERSON ACCEPTS THE CARD AND USES IT, THEN THE CONSUMER, IN EFFECT, ACCEPTS THE TERMS AND CONDITIONS OF THE CREDIT COMPANY. WHEN A PERSON REQUESTS OR ACCEPTS A CREDIT CARD, HE IS LIABLE FOR THE FIRST $50.00 (THIS MAY VARY) OF ITS UNAUTHORIZED USE. THIS LIABILITY CAN BE ERASED IF THE CARD OWNER IS ABLE TO NOTIFY THE CREDITOR OF THE CARD'S LOSS BEFORE ANY UNAUTHORIZED USE OF THE CARD OCCURS.

74

- GARNISHMENT -

IN ORDER TO SATISFY AN UNPAID DEBT, CREDITORS ARE ALLOWED TO MAKE AN ATTACHMENT, OR GARNISHMENT, ON A DEBTOR'S WAGES. ACCORDING TO A SECTION OF THE CONSUMER CREDIT PROTECTION ACT KNOWN AS TITLE III, GARNISHMENT CAN ONLY BE IMPOSED WITH THE CONSENT OF THE DEBTOR OR THOUGH A COURT ORDER. TITLE III ALSO LIMITS GARNISHMENT TO 25 PERCENT OF THE DEBTOR'S DISPOSABLE INCOME, OR EVEN LESS DEPENDING ON THE GARNISHMENT LAWS OF THE VARIOUS STATES. FINALLY, TITLE III FORBIDS EMPLOYERS FROM FIRING AN EMPLOYEE SIMPLY BECAUSE HIS WAGES ARE BEING GARNISHED.

BANKRUPTCY

CONSUMERS WHO FIND THEMSELVES IN THE UNHAPPY POSITION OF BEING UNABLE TO PAY THEIR BILLS MAY SEEK PROTECTION FROM THEIR CREDITORS THROUGH FEDERAL BANKRUPTCY PROCEEDINGS. HISTORICALLY, BANKRUPTCY HAS MEANT LIQUIDATING **ALL** OF ONE'S ASSETS TO SATISFY THEIR DEBTS. TODAY, HOWEVER, DEBTORS ARE PERMITTED TO RETAIN POSSESSION OF A GOOD PORTION OF THEIR POSSESSIONS AND REAL ESTATE SO THAT THEY ARE NOT HOMELESS AND DESTITUTE. BANKRUPTCY RULES ARE NOW HEAVILY TILTED TOWARD THE DEBTOR TO THE DEGREE THAT A PERSON CAN OFTEN BENEFIT FROM DECLARING BANKRUPTCY AND NO LONGER FEEL THE SOCIAL STIGMATISM ATTACHED TO THE WORD.

CASE STUDY
- BANKRUPTCY -

ONE DAY JERN SPOLD BECAME CONVINCED THAT SOON THE WORLD WOULD BE PLAGUED BY HOUSEHOLD APPLIANCES THAT HAD INEXPLICABLY BECOME EMBEDDED IN THE EARTH'S CRUST. JERN FELT THE NEED TO BE READY.

TO THAT END SPOLD BORROWED HEAVILY TO START HIS OWN BUSINESS HE EVEN TRAINED AN EXPERT STAFF.

"OKAY, WHO WANTS TO PULL THIS BABY OUT?"

"I WILL"

UNFORTUNATELY, REPORTED INCIDENTS OF EMBEDDED APPLIANCES WERE NOT COMING IN. JERN WAS FACED WITH AN IMMEDIATE PAYROLL CRISIS...

"LOOK, WOULD ANY OF YOU GUYS CONSIDER - WORKING ON A COMMISSION BASIS?"

AS HIS DREAM CRUMBLED AND CREDITORS BEGAN TO SWARM, JERN'S WIFE OFFERED SOUND ADVICE.

JERN, JERN. FILE FOR BANKRUPTCY. LOOK, SOME DAY THE APPLIANCE REMOVAL INDUSTRY WILL SPRING UP AND YOU'LL COMMAND FAT FEES AS A CONSULTANT.

THE NEXT DAY JERN FILED, IN FEDERAL DISTRICT COURT, A PETITION TO DECLARE HIMSELF BANKRUPT.

BANKRUPTCY COURT PROCEEDINGS

WITH HIS LAWYER TO ADVISE HIM, JERN SAT DOWN AND LISTED ALL HIS PERSONAL ASSETS, AND/OR PROPERTY THAT HE ALONE OWNED AND WHERE IT WAS LOCATED AND THE ESTIMATED VALUE OF ALL HIS ASSETS. HE THEN LISTED ALL OF HIS CREDITORS AND THE AMOUNTS HE OWED THEM. THIS CONSTITUTED JERN'S PETITION FOR BANKRUPTCY. JERN THEN APPEARED BEFORE A FEDERAL DISTRICT JUDGE AND ATTESTED TO THE VALIDITY OF THE PETITION. THE JUDGE THEN DECLARED JERN BANKRUPT. A TRUSTEE WAS APPOINTED TO LIQUIDATE JERN'S ASSETS AND DISTRIBUTE THE MONIES PROPORTIONATELY TO JERN'S CREDITORS. AS A BANKRUPT, JERN WAS DISCHARGED OF ANY DEBT HE LISTED NOT COVERED BY HIS STATED ASSETS.

"MY ASSETS, WHEN LIQUIDATED, ONLY COVERED HALF OF WHAT I OWED, BUT YOU'RE SAYING I WON'T HAVE TO PAY THAT OTHER HALF EVER?"

"RIGHT- NOT SO LONG AS - YOU LISTED THOSE DEBTS AND THEY ARE DISCHARGEABLE."

A DAY LATER

"SAY, MY MOM JUST SENT ME A CHECK FOR $5000.⁰⁰ DO I HAVE TO TURN THAT MONEY OVER TO THE CREDITORS ON MY PETITION?"

LEGALLY...NO.

CHAPTER SIX

CRIMINAL LAW & THE CRIMINAL JUSTICE SYSTEM

1379 B

SOCIETY CREATES LAWS TO PROTECT PEOPLE FROM INJURY OR LOSS CAUSED BY THE THE WRONGFUL ACTS OF OTHERS. AT THE SAME TIME SOCIETY TRIES TO PROTECT THOSE ACCUSED WHO MAY, IN FACT, BE INNOCENT. THIS BALANCE BETWEEN THE PROTECTION OF SOCIETY FROM CRIMINALS AND THE RIGHTS OF THE ACCUSED IS WHAT THE CRIMINAL JUSTICE SYSTEM IS ALL ABOUT.

TYPES of CRIMES

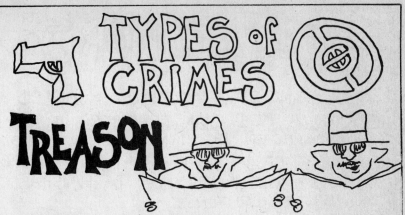

TREASON

TREASON IS A CRIME
AGAINST THE GOVERNMENT. A PERSON CON-
VICTED OF TREASON IS GUILTY OF ATTEMPT-
ING EITHER TO OVERTHROW THE GOVERN-
MENT OR TO BETRAY IT TO AN ENEMY POWER.

FELONY

FELONIES ARE SERIOUS CRIMES THAT ARE
PUNISHABLE BY IMPRISONMENT AND STEEP
FINES. SOME FELONIES, SUCH AS MURDER, ARE
CAPITAL CRIMES & ARE PUNISHABLE BY DEATH IN SOME STATES.

MISTER, IF YOU SHOOT ME
THAT'LL BE A FELONY
WITH A CAPITAL "F"
AND "F" RHYMES
WITH DEATH,
WHICH IS WHAT
YOU GET.

MISDEMEANORS

MISDEMEANORS ARE GENERALLY MUCH **LESS SERIOUS** CRIMES THAN FELONIES. USUALLY, MISDEMEANORS ARE PUNISHABLE BY FINES AND/OR PROBATION. HOWEVER, SOME MORE SERIOUS MISDEMEANORS MAY BE PUNISHABLE BY A BRIEF SENTENCE.

THIRTY DAYS IN PRISON?! FOR DRUNK & DISORDERLY CONDUCT!? JUDGE, YOU'VE GOT TO BE KIDDING.

MR. KRENDALL, YOU'VE PUT IN PLENTY OF TIME PROPPING YOURSELF UP IN EVERY BAR IN TOWN, I DON'T SEE HOW IT COULD HURT IF YOU PUT IN A LITTLE TIME **BEHIND** BARS FOR A CHANGE.

THE TERMS "FELONY" AND "MISDEMEANOR" ARE USED TO DESCRIBE THE SEVERITY OF THE CRIME. THERE ARE OTHER WAYS TO CATEGORIZE CRIMES.

CRIMES AGAINST PROPERTY

PEOPLE COMMIT CRIMES AGAINST EITHER PEOPLE OR THEIR PROPERTY. THE FOLLOWING ARE THE MOST COMMON CRIMES AGAINST PROPERTY.

ARSON

ARSON IS A VERY SERIOUS CRIME. AN ARSON-IST IS SOMEONE WHO STARTS A FIRE ON SOMEONE'S PROPERTY OR IN THEIR BUILDING. JUST LIKE MURDER, ARSON IS A CRIME WITH DIFFERENT DEGREES OF SEVERITY. FOR EXAMPLE, FIRST-DEGREE ARSON WOULD BE SETTING A FIRE IN A BUILDING WHEN PEOPLE ARE INSIDE AND THEIR LIVES ARE EN-DANGERED. SECOND-DEGREE ARSON, SOME-TIMES REFERRED TO AS "SON OF ARSON", IS BURNING DOWN A VACANT BUILDING. THIRD-DEGREE ARSON IS A LESSER CRIME WHERE SOMEONE STARTS A FIRE IN A CAR OR ANY OTHER TYPE OF PROPERTY THAT HAS A VALUE OF AT LEAST $25.00.

LARGENY

LARCENY IS SIMPLY TAKING ANOTHER'S PROP-
ERTY AND INTENDING TO DEPRIVE THEM OF IT
PERMANENTLY.

BURGLARY

A BURGLAR IS SOMEONE WHO BREAKS INTO
ANOTHER'S HOUSE WITH THE INTENT TO COMMIT A
CRIME WHEN THE PEOPLE AREN'T AT HOME OR
ARE FAST ASLEEP.

RECEIVING STOLEN GOODS

IF SOMEONE KNOWINGLY RECEIVES STOLEN PROPERTY THEN THEY ARE GUILTY OF A FELONY.

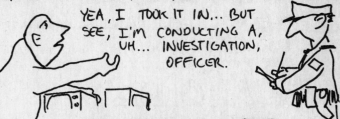

YEA, I TOOK IT IN... BUT SEE, I'M CONDUCTING A, UH... INVESTIGATION, OFFICER.

FORGERY

FORGING, OR COUNTERFEITING, SOMEONE ELSE'S SIGNATURE OR ALTERING ANOTHER'S WRITING IN SUCH A WAY AS TO DEPRIVE THAT PERSON OF HIS PROPERTY OR RIGHT IS A FELONY.

WAIT... I'M THE BONA FIDE ORIGINAL... I CAN PROVE IT! REMEMBER THAT DAY YOU SLOPPED COFFEE ON ME? I'VE STILL GOT THE WATER MARK TO PROVE IT.

CRIMES AGAINST THE PERSON

WE HAVE SEEN A FEW CRIMES AGAINST PROPERTY. NOW WE'LL LOOK AT SOME CRIMES AGAINST THE PERSON.

HOMICIDE

HOMICIDE IS THE ACT OF TAKING ANOTHER'S LIFE. HOMICIDE COMES IN ALL SIZES...

LEGAL HOMICIDE

WHEN THE STATE PUTS A PRISONER TO DEATH, THE EXECUTIONER IS SAID TO PERFORM A LEGAL HOMICIDE.

JUSTIFIABLE HOMICIDE

WHEN A POLICE OFFICER MUST TAKE ANOTHER'S LIFE IN THE LINE OF DUTY IT IS OFTEN CONSIDERED JUSTIFIABLE OR EXCUSABLE HOMICIDE. ALSO, IF SOMEONE IS ACTING IN SELF-DEFENSE, THE HOMICIDE HE COMMITS MAY BE CONSIDERED JUSTIFIABLE.

ACCIDENTAL HOMICIDE

THIS IS A PURELY ACCIDENTAL DEATH CAUSED BY SOMEONE WHO, EVEN THOUGH ACTING LEGALLY AND RESPONSIBLY, SOMEHOW CAUSES THE DEATH OF ANOTHER.

CRACK

MANSLAUGHTER

MANSLAUGHTER IS A FORM OF ACCIDENTAL DEATH, BUT IT IS THE RESULT OF NEGLIGENCE OR OCCURS AS A RESULT OF SUDDEN VIOLENCE SUCH AS MIGHT HAPPEN IN A HEATED ARGUMENT. UNLIKE MURDER, MANSLAUGHTER IS NOT CONSIDERED INTENTIONAL.

MURDER

MURDER ISN'T JUST TAKING ANOTHER PERSON'S LIFE. MURDER, IN THE FIRST DEGREE, IS PLANNING AND TAKING ACTION THAT THE KILLER KNOWS WILL, AND INTENDS TO, RESULT IN THE DEATH OF ANOTHER. MURDER, OF COURSE, IS A FELONY AND IN SOME STATES A CAPITAL CRIME PUNISHABLE BY DEATH.

MORE CRIMES AGAINST THE PERSON...
KIDNAPPING

KIDNAPPING IS HOLDING SOMEONE AGAINST HIS WILL. IN SOME STATES, KIDNAPPING IS A CAPITAL CRIME — THAT IS, EVEN IF THE KIDNAPPED PERSON IS RETURNED SAFELY, THE KIDNAPPERS MAY STILL FACE THE DEATH SENTENCE.

ROBBERY

ROBBERY IS TAKING SOMEONES PERSONAL POSSESSIONS EITHER AT GUNPOINT OR BY SOME OTHER THREAT OF PERSONAL VIOLENCE.

EXTORTION

AN EXTORTIONIST OBTAINS MONEY FROM OTHERS THROUGH THE USE OF FEAR OR FORCE. BLACKMAIL IS ONE FORM OF EXTORTION.

PERJURY

PERJURY IS LYING UNDER OATH. PEOPLE WHO PERJURE THEMSELVES MAY DO SO TO PROTECT A GUILTY PERSON OR INCRIMINATE AN INNOCENT PERSON. EITHER WAY, PERJURY IS A FELONY.

CRIMINAL CAPACITY

THE LAW STATES THAT A PERSON MUST HAVE THE CAPACITY TO COMMIT A CRIME IN ORDER TO BE PUNISHED FOR THAT CRIME, EVEN IF THERE IS PROOF POSITIVE THAT THE PERSON COMMITTED THE CRIME. THIS IS MEANT TO PROTECT MINORS OR MENTALLY RETARDED PEOPLE WHO MAY HAVE COMMITTED A CRIME WITHOUT REALIZING THAT WHAT THEY HAVE DONE IS WRONG OR WHAT THE CONSEQUENCES OF THEIR ACTION MAY BE.

"CUT THE BABY ACT. YOU DID IT... WE KNOW YOU DID IT... AND MOST IMPORTANT YOU KNOW - YOU DID IT!"

MINORS CAN BE TRIED FOR CRIMES AS ADULTS IF IT CAN BE SHOWN THAT THE MINOR HAD CRIMINAL CAPACITY AND UNDERSTOOD THE CONSEQUENCES OF HIS ACTIONS.

INTENT

IN CRIMINAL LAW, INTENT IS THE CEMENT WHICH HOLDS THE BRICKS TOGETHER. A PERSON MAY BUY A GUN WITHOUT INTENT TO COMMIT A CRIME. HOWEVER, IF THAT PERSON POINTS THAT GUN AT SOMEONE AND DEMANDS MONEY, THEN HIS INTENTION TO COMMIT A CRIME WITH THAT GUN IS QUITE CLEAR.

MOTIVE

MOTIVE IS THE WHY OF CRIME. IN MOST CASES MOTIVE IS APPARENT AND CAN POINT THE FINGER OF BLAME. HOWEVER, SOME PEOPLE COMMIT CRIMES AGAINST OTHERS WITHOUT ANY CLEAR MOTIVE OR REASON. THEREFORE, IN CRIMINAL LAW IT IS MORE IMPORTANT TO ESTABLISH INTENT THAN TO FIND MOTIVE.

INSANITY

THE INSANITY DEFENSE, WHEN ALLOWED, REVOLVES AROUND THE QUESTIONS OF INTENT, CAPACITY AND MOTIVE. SOME STATES CONTEND THAT A SANE PERSON CAN BECOME TEMPORARILY INSANE, OR UNABLE TO KNOW THE DIFFERENCE BETWEEN RIGHT AND WRONG, AND SO LACK THE CAPACITY TO COMMIT THE CRIME. IN SUCH CASES, THE DEFENDANT, THOUGH CLEARLY GUILTY, IS DECLARED "NOT GUILTY BY REASON OF INSANITY." HE IS THEN SENT TO A PSYCHIATRIC HOSPITAL FOR TREATMENT.

CRIMINAL COURTROOM PROCEDURE

IF A CRIME HAS BEEN COMMITTED AND THE POLICE HAVE A SUSPECT IN MIND, THE POLICE MUST APPEAR BEFORE A JUDGE AND EXPLAIN WHY THEY SUSPECT THIS PARTICULAR PERSON. THE JUDGE MAY THEN ISSUE EITHER A SUMMONS OR A BENCH WARRANT. A SUMMONS IS A DOCUMENT SENT TO THE ACCUSED THAT CALLS HIM INTO COURT. A WARRANT IS FOR MORE SERIOUS CRIMES. A WARRANT IS AN ARREST ORDER THAT GIVES THE POLICE THE RIGHT TO APPREHEND THE ACCUSED AND BRING HIM IN. A SUSPECT BROUGHT IN WILL BE QUESTIONED BY THE POLICE. BEFORE QUESTIONING, THE ACCUSED MUST BE READ HIS "MIRANDA" RIGHTS.

"OKAY, SON, I'LL READ IT JUST ONCE MORE... YOU HAVE THE RIGHT TO REMAIN SILENT, ANYTHING YOU SAY CAN AND WILL BE USED AGAINST YOU, YOU HAVE THE RIGHT TO AN ATTORNEY. IF YOU CANNOT AFFORD AN ATTORNEY... "

ARRAIGNMENT

ARRAIGNMENT IS A FORMAL COURTROOM PROCEDURE WHERE AN ACCUSED IS BROUGHT BEFORE A JUDGE AND INFORMED OF THE CHARGES AGAINST HIM. AT THIS POINT THE ACCUSED WOULD DO WELL TO HIRE A LAWYER. HOWEVER, SHOULD THE ACCUSED BE UNABLE TO AFFORD A LAWYER, HE MAY ASK THE COURT TO APPOINT ONE FOR HIM.

INDICTMENT

THE INDICTMENT IS A LEGAL DOCUMENT, PREPARED BY THE PROSECUTOR, WHICH IS HANDED DOWN IN AN ARRAIGNMENT PROCEEDING SPECIFICALLY NAMING THE ACCUSED AND SETTING DOWN THE CHARGES AGAINST HIM. THE ACCUSED MUST THEN ENTER HIS PLEA TO THE CHARGES AGAINST HIM.

HOW DO YOU PLEAD... GUILTY OR NOT GUILTY?

. GUILTY OR NOT GUILTY? YOU DON'T GIVE A GUY MANY OPTIONS... HOW ABOUT WE SAY, GUILTY, NOT GUILTY OR I TAKE WHATS BEHIND DOOR NUMBER THREE! AND I TAKE WHAT'S BEHIND DOOR NUMBER THREE.

ALL RIGHT, BAILIFF. TELL THE DEFENDANT WHAT IS BEHIND DOOR NUMBER THREE.

BEHIND DOOR NUMBER THREE WE HAVE A CONTEMPT OF COURT CITATION.

PRESUMPTION of INNOCENCE

THE CONSTITUTIONAL HALLMARK OF THE CRIMINAL JUSTICE SYSTEM IS THAT THE ACCUSED IS PRESUMED INNOCENT UNTIL PROVEN GUILTY.

"I GOTTA HAND IT TO YOU KILLER, THE HALO... THE MOTHER TERESA GARB,... NOT A JURY IN THE WORLD IS GONNA CONVICT YA."

PLEA BARGAINING

BECAUSE OF THE ENORMOUS NUMBER OF CRIMINAL TRIALS THAT ARE BACK-LOGGED IN MOST MAJOR CITIES, PROSECUTORS SOMETIMES SEEK TO ELIMINATE TRIALS BY ENCOURAGING DEFENDANTS TO PLEAD GUILTY, NOT TO THE CRIME THEY ARE ACCUSED OF BUT TO A LESSER CHARGE FOR A LIGHTER PUNISHMENT. PLEA BARGAINING MAY REDUCE THE WORK LOAD FOR PROSECUTORS AND ASSURE CONVICTIONS, BUT IT ALSO ALLOWS GUILTY PEOPLE TO ESCAPE SERIOUS PUNISHMENT.

TODAY'S
BARGAIN
BURGLARY
MARKED DOWN
TO
LARCENY!

SPEEDY TRIAL

HOW DO YOU PLEAD, SON?

EXHAUSTED

THE CONSTITUTION ALSO GUARANTEES THAT THE ACCUSED RECEIVE A SPEEDY TRIAL. WHAT IS MEANT BY A SPEEDY TRIAL IS HARD TO SAY, OTHER THAN A TRIAL WITHOUT UNNECESSARY DELAYS. BUT EVERY TRIAL HAS ITS OWN SPECIAL COMPLICATIONS, MAKING IT VERY DIFFICULT TO DETERMINE IF SOMEONE IS BEING DENIED HIS RIGHT TO A SPEEDY TRIAL.

TIME LIMITS

EACH STATE IMPOSES LIMITATIONS ON THE AMOUNT OF TIME PROSECUTORS HAVE TO PROSECUTE VARIOUS CRIMES. HOWEVER, THERE ARE NO TIME LIMITS ON THE CRIME OF MURDER AND IN MOST CASES ON THE CRIME OF KIDNAPPING.

DOUBLE JEOPARDY

IN A SENSE, JEOPARDY MEANS TROUBLE—
THE TROUBLE A PERSON IS IN WHEN HE
IS TRIED FOR A CRIME. DOUBLE JEOPARDY,
THEN, IN CRIMINAL LAW, IS THE JEOPARDY
A PERSON IS IN WHEN HE IS TRIED
FOR THE SAME CRIME FOR A SECOND TIME.
AS SUCH, DOUBLE JEOPARDY IS FORBIDDEN
IN CRIMINAL LAW.

97

SENTENCING

WHEN A DEFENDANT HAS PLED GUILTY OR BEEN FOUND GUILTY BY A JURY, THE TRIAL JUDGE MUST THEN DETERMINE WHAT THE PUNISHMENT SHALL BE. SOME STATES GIVE THE JUDGE A LOT OF DISCRETION, OR LEEWAY, IN DETERMINING HOW LONG A PRISON SENTENCE (WITHIN CERTAIN LIMITATIONS) TO GIVE, WHILE OTHER STATES MANDATE SPECIFIC SENTENCES FOR EACH CRIME.

10 YEARS

PAROLE

MOST PRISONERS ARE ELIGIBLE FOR PAROLE BEFORE THEY HAVE SERVED THEIR FULL SENTENCE. PAROLE IS AN AGREEMENT BETWEEN THE PRISONER AND THE STATE THAT ALLOWS THE PRISONER TO GAIN EARLY RELEASE ON THE CONDITION THAT HE NO LONGER ENGAGE IN CRIMINAL ACTIVITIES. SHOULD THE PAROLEE BREAK HIS PROMISE, HE MUST FACE A PAROLE BOARD. THE BOARD MAY DECIDE TO GIVE THE PAROLEE ANOTHER CHANCE OR THEY MAY RETURN HIM TO PRISON WITHOUT A TRIAL.

CASE STUDY

ON JUNE 3rd 198- WILLIS GOLP INFORMED HIS WIFE THAT SHE ANNOYED HIM.

"I MEAN, YOU REALLY GET MY GOAT."

A HEATED EXCHANGE FOLLOWED, LEADING TO BLOWS AND ENDING IN MR. GOLP'S BLUDGEONING HIS WIFE TO DEATH.

ANNOYING, GLADYS... REAL ANNOYING.

MR. GOLP THEN DISPOSED OF MRS. GOLP IN THE INCINERATOR.

SO LONG, GLADYS.

MR. GOLP THEN PHONED THE POLICE AND REPORT-
ED THAT HIS WIFE WAS MISSING, THAT SHE HAD NOT
RETURNED FROM A WALK AROUND THE BLOCK. WHEN
QUESTIONED BY A DETECTIVE, MR. GOLP ACTED VERY
STRANGE.

"HA HA HA!
SHE JUST DIDN'T
COME HOME. HO
HO. WHAT DO YOU
MAKE OF THAT?"

THE POLICE WANTED TO CHARGE MR. GOLP WITH MURDER,
BUT WITHOUT A BODY, A MURDER WEAPON OR EVEN
A CONFESSION, IT WOULD BE A TOUGH CASE TO PRO-
SECUTE. AN INVESTIGATION TURNED UP BLOOD STAINS
THAT MATCHED MRS. GOLP'S BLOOD TYPE. A SET OF
DENTURES AND A RING WITH MRS. GOLP'S INITIALS
WERE FOUND IN THE INCINERATOR. QUESTIONING
THE NEIGHBORS, THE POLICE LEARNED THAT THE GOLPS
HAD A HISTORY OF BELTING IT OUT. MR. GOLP
WAS ARRAIGNED ON FIRST-DEGREE MURDER
CHARGES. FACING A POSSIBLE DEATH ROW CONVICTION,
MR. GOLP CONFESSED TO MURDER BUT NOT
MURDER IN THE FIRST DEGREE.

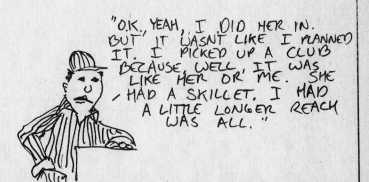

"O.K., YEAH, I DID HER IN.
BUT IT WASN'T LIKE I PLANNED
IT. I PICKED UP A CLUB
BECAUSE, WELL, IT WAS
LIKE HER OR ME. SHE
HAD A SKILLET. I HAD
A LITTLE LONGER REACH
WAS ALL."

BY CONFESSING TO SECOND-DEGREE MURDER, MR.
GOLP WAS SENTENCED TO LIFE IN PRISON. BUT NOT
ON DEATH ROW.

CHAPTER SEVEN

MARRIAGE

& DIVORCE

THE ACT OF MARRIAGE IS REALLY NOTHING MORE THAN A CEREMONY, SACRED OR OTHERWISE. BUT THERE IS SOMETHING KNOWN AS THE MARRIAGE CONTRACT. THE MARRIAGE CONTRACT IS MORE THAN SACRED... IT'S LEGALLY BINDING. LIKE MOST OTHER CONTRACTS THE MARRIAGE CONTRACT OBLIGATES TWO PEOPLE TO PERFORM CERTAIN DUTIES IN EXCHANGE FOR SOME CONSIDERATION. BUT, UNLIKE OTHER CONTRACTS, THE MARRIAGE CONTRACT IS IRREVOCABLE BY EITHER PARTY **UNLESS** THERE IS A SPECIFIC DECREE GRANTED BY THE COURTS.

AND DO YOU PROMISE TO LOVE, HONOR AND CHERISH HER AND TO DELIVER TO HER COMPANY 30,000 HOG BELLIES ACCORDING TO THE TERMS OF THIS JOINT CONTRACT... SO HELP YOU GOD?

I DO.

LEGAL CONTRACTS PERFORMED ~ HERE ~

TODAY'S SPECIAL for **ONE** TWO

103

THE LEGAL TIES THAT BIND

UNTIL FAIRLY RECENTLY COMMON LAW STATED THAT MAN AND WIFE WERE ONE, AND THAT THE MAN WAS HEAD OF THE HOUSEHOLD, WHICH MEANT HE ALONE HELD TITLE TO ALL MARITAL POSSESSIONS. TODAY, THE COURTS STILL CONSIDER THE HUSBAND TO BE THE HEAD OF THE HOUSEHOLD, AND AS SUCH HE MAY BE LEGALLY OBLIGATED TO PROVIDE FOR HIS WIFE AND FAMILY. AS FOR THE WIFE, SHE IS, TODAY, CONSIDERED LEGALLY QUALIFIED TO ENTER INTO HER OWN CONTRACTS AND TO SUE OR BE SUED. HER LEGAL OBLIGATIONS TO HER HUSBAND ARE STILL CONSIDERED TO BE MAINTAINING THE HOME AND OTHER SERVICES. IN FACT, A HUSBAND CAN SUE FOR DAMAGES IF 'HIS WIFE IS NO LONGER ABLE TO PROVIDE THESE SERVICES SHOULD SHE BE INJURED OR KILLED IN AN ACCIDENT.

THE VALID MARRIAGE

EVERY STATE HAS ITS OWN LAWS AS TO WHO CAN LEGALLY MARRY. MANY STATES DO NOT PERMIT MINORS TO MARRY UNLESS THEY HAVE PARENTAL CONSENT. MANY STATES DO NOT ALLOW BLOOD RELATIVES TO MARRY EACH OTHER, AND SEVERAL STATES RESTRICT MARRIAGES BETWEEN MENTALLY INCOMPETENT PEOPLE. MOST STATES DONT HOLD A MARRIAGE TO BE LEGALLY BINDING UNTIL IT IS CONSUMMATED. SHOULD THE HUSBAND PROVE TO BE IMPOTENT, THE WIFE MAY HAVE THE MARRIAGE ANNULED. (STERILITY, OF EITHER SPOUSE, IS NOT A GROUND FOR ANNULMENT.)

"MAYBE IF WE BOTH LOST A LITTLE WEIGHT."

COMMON·LAW MARRIAGE

SEVERAL STATES RECOGNIZE THE COMMON-LAW MARRIAGE. THIS IS A LEGAL STATE OF MARRIAGE CREATED BETWEEN MAN AND WIFE WITHOUT THE BENEFIT OF CEREMONY, LICENSE OR ANY OTHER LEGAL FORMALITY.

IT IS BASED SIMPLY ON THE COUPLE'S PRACTICE OF LIVING TOGETHER AS MAN AND WIFE FOR A CERTAIN NUMBER OF YEARS (EACH STATE VARIES, BUT USUALLY THE PERIOD IS SEVEN YEARS).

WELL, SEVEN YEARS TO THE MINUTE. THAT'LL DO IT... SO HONEY, HOW DOES IT FEEL NOW THAT WE'RE MAN AND WIFE?

FINALLY! O.K. SO WE DIDN'T HAVE TO RENT A HALL AND PAY A CATERER, BUT SEVEN YEARS IS A LONG TIME TO BE STANDING HERE IN THIS CRUMMY GOWN...

BREACH OF PROMISE...

IF MARRIAGE IS A LEGAL CONTRACT, OF SORTS, THEN THE OFFER OF MARRIAGE AND ITS ACCEPTANCE MIGHT BE CONSIDERED A VALID CONTRACT. IN FACT, THE COURTS TOOK THIS POSITION UNTIL VERY RECENTLY, WHEN IT BECAME APPARENT THAT SUCH CASES WERE DIFFICULT TO PROVE AND OFTEN PHONY.

TELL ME, HUBERT, WHAT SORT OF WOMAN WOULD YOU WANT TO MARRY YOU?

TO MARRY ME..?

WHAT?! OH YES, HUBERT, YES, OH, HUBERT, I'M SO, SO HAPPY...

WHAT??

YOUR OFFER OF MARRIAGE, AND I ACCEPT.

BUT LYDIA, DEAR, I WAS MERELY RESPONDING...

CONGRATULATIONS, HUBERT. MAY I BE THE FIRST.

OH, DADDY, ISN'T IT WONDERFUL!

MR. WHITE! WHERE DID YOU COME FROM?

BUT I DON'T....

JUST HAPPENING BY, SON, LET ME SHAKE YOUR HAND..

BUT HUBERT, WE DID HEAR YOU PROPOSE.

YES WE DID.

MARRIAGE
ON THE ROCKS

WHEN TWO PEOPLE CANNOT REMAIN TOGETHER, FOR WHATEVER REASON, THEY MAY SEEK TO END THEIR MARRIAGE. DIVORCE, OR SOME VARIATION THEREOF (ANNULMENT, DISSOLUTION & SEPARATION), IS RARELY A SIMPLE PROCEDURE AND MUST ALWAYS BE APPROVED BY THE COURTS. WHILE A FEW STATES USE THE WORD "DIVORCE" TO BRING AN END TO ANY MARRIAGE, MOST STATES BREAK DIVORCE DOWN INTO SPECIFIC CATEGORIES.

ANNULMENT

ANNULMENT DECLARES A MARRIAGE VOID, OR NEVER HAVING BEEN VALID IN THE FIRST PLACE. ANNULMENT ERASES ANY RECORD OF THE MARRIAGE WITH THE COURT. COURTS GRANT ANNULMENT IN CASES WHERE ONE OR BOTH SPOUSES WERE UNDER AGE OR LEGALLY INCOMPETENT OR IF THE MARRIAGE WAS PERFORMED UNDER DURESS OR OTHER FRAUDULENT CIRCUMSTANCES.

"LYDIA, I HAVE A CONFESSION TO MAKE."

"ME TOO!"

108

DISSOLUTION

DISSOLUTION IS JUST ANOTHER WORD FOR DIVORCE - OR RATHER, DIVORCE UNDER SPECIAL CIRCUMSTANCES. STATES THAT PERMIT DISSOLUTION DO SO WHEN ONE SPOUSE BECOMES INCURABLY INSANE OR GOES TO PRISON FOR A LIFE SENTENCE OR SOME OTHER UNFORTUNATE REASON. SOME STATES ALSO PERMIT DISSOLUTION UNDER A PROCEEDING KNOWN AS **ENOCH ARDEN.** THIS IS USED TO DISSOLVE A MARRIAGE WHEN ONE SPOUSE VANISHES AND DISAPPEARS WITHOUT A TRACE.

INVISIBLE MAN

" TWO PLEASE... MY FORMER HUSBAND MAY NOT BE VISIBLE BUT HE STILL INSISTS ON PAYING HIS WAY... "

SEPARATION

SEPARATION IS SORT OF A TRIAL DIVORCE. WITH DIVORCE, ALL LEGAL TIES ARE SEVERED, THERE IS NO RECONCILIATION AND NO TURNING BACK, EXCEPT THROUGH REMARRIAGE. BUT WITH SEPARATION, MAN AND WIFE CAN LIVE APART (AND YET STILL MAINTAIN CERTAIN MARITAL OBLIGATIONS). ALSO, IF THERE IS A RECONCILIATION, THE SEPARATION AGREEMENT IS SIMPLY THROWN AWAY AND THE COUPLE REMAINS MARRIED. THE SEPARATION AGREEMENT, USUALLY WORKED OUT BY THE LAWYERS, PROVIDES FOR ALIMONY AND CHILD SUPPORT JUST AS A DIVORCE DECREE WOULD WITHOUT THE FINALITY OF A DIVORCE.

FOR THE SAKE OF OUR MARRIAGE, CLAUDIA AND I SEPARATE TWO OR THREE TIMES A YEAR.

DIVORCE

DIVORCE HAS BEEN CALLED THE LAST WORD IN MARRIAGE. IT CAN BE ONE OF THE MOST COMPLEX OF LEGAL PROCEEDINGS OR IT CAN BE ONE OF THE SIMPLEST, AND LATELY IT HAS BECOME ONE OF THE MOST COMMON.

"HOT DOGS! PEANUTS! DIVORCE DECREES - HERE!"

SINCE THE COURTS CONSIDER THE FAMILY TO BE THE FABRIC OF SOCIETY, AND MARRIAGE TO BE THE BASIS OF THE FAMILY, THEY HAVE LONG TRIED TO MAKE GETTING A DIVORCE AS DIFFICULT AS POSSIBLE. THIS IS WHY THE COURTS HAVE ALWAYS DEMANDED SOME BASIS, OR GROUNDS, BEFORE GRANTING A DIVORCE.

GROUNDS for DIVORCE

WHILE ALL STATES VARY IN RULES REGARDING DIVORCE PROCEEDINGS, THE FOLLOWING GROUNDS ARE GENERALLY ACCEPTED NATIONWIDE.

ADULTERY

A NO-NO SINCE THE DAYS OF MOSES AND THE TEN COMMANDMENTS, THIS GROUND WILL DO IT ALMOST EVERY TIME.

CRUELTY

EVERY STATE DEFINES CRUELTY A LITTLE DIFFERENTLY. HOWEVER, IN RECENT YEARS ALL STATES HAVE BROADENED THEIR DEFINITION.

DESERTION

SOMETIMES REFERRED TO AS THE POOR MAN'S
DIVORCE. DESERTION IS A FORM OF SEPARATION
THAT IS (NEITHER VOLUNTARY) NOR GRANTED BY A
COURT. IN DESERTION, ONE SPOUSE
SIMPLY ABANDONS THE OTHER. A DIVORCE DECREE
PROVIDING FOR ALIMONY AND CHILD SUPPORT CAN
BE GRANTED IN CASES OF DESERTION, BUT IT MAY BE
DIFFICULT TO ENFORCE IF THE DESERTING
SPOUSE HAS FLED WITHOUT A TRACE.

INCOMPATIBILITY

ALSO KNOWN AS IRRECONCILABLE DIFFERENCES.
THIS IS A SORT OF NO-FAULT DIVORCE,
WHICH MOST STATES NOW PROVIDE FOR.
NO-FAULT DIVORCE ISN'T NECESSARILY CLEAN
AND SIMPLE DIVORCE, IT'S JUST THAT NEITHER
SIDE IS CONTESTING THE DIVORCE SO ALL THAT
REMAINS IS THE SETTLEMENT.

O.K., I GET THE HOUSE,
THE CAR & THE KIDS
AND YOU GET THE REST...

TERRIFIC, I GET THE
MORTGAGE, THE CAR
PAYMENTS AND THE
CHILD SUPPORT!
WHAT A DEAL!

ALIMONY

ALIMONY IS SUPPORT MONEY ORDERED BY THE COURT TO BE PAID BY ONE SPOUSE TO ANOTHER OUT OF INCOME OR HOLDINGS IN SETTLEMENT OF EITHER A DIVORCE OR A SEPARATION PROCEEDING. FAILURE TO PAY ALIMONY IS A CONTEMPT OF COURT ACTION AND IS PUNISHABLE BY FINES AND IMPRISONMENT.

CUSTODY of CHILDREN

IN A DIVORCE SETTLEMENT IT IS THE COURT'S OBLIGATION TO DETERMINE WHICH PARENT SHOULD BE AWARDED CUSTODY OF THE CHILDREN. MOST OFTEN THE MOTHER IS GRANTED CUSTODY. HOWEVER, THAT IS CHANGING. TODAY, THE COURTS ARE TRYING TO BE FAIR TO BOTH PARENTS AND PARTICULARLY THE CHILD WHO IS OFTEN ASKED TO STATE HIS OR HER PREFERENCE.

DO-IT-YOURSELF
DIVORCE

THERE ARE SEVERAL STATES THAT PERMIT A DO-IT-YOURSELF DIVORCE WITHOUT THE AID OR EXPENSE OF A LAWYER. SO LONG AS THE PROPER LEGAL FORMS ARE OBTAINED AND FILED CORRECTLY AND THE COURTROOM PROCEDURE IS UNDERSTOOD, THIS IS A VERY PAINLESS WAY TO OBTAIN A DIVORCE. HOWEVER, COURT CLERKS AND JUDGES ARE NOT PERMITTED TO DISPENSE LEGAL ADVICE AND JUDGES HAVE BEEN KNOWN TO DENY DIVORCES TO PEOPLE WHO ARE NOT PREPARED. THE BEST WAY TO PREPARE FOR A DO-IT-YOURSELF DIVORCE IS TO ATTEND SIMILAR TRIALS AND OBSERVE OTHERS DOING IT.

CASE STUDY I DIVORCE

MARGE AND FULTON CLUTZ HAVE BEEN MARRIED FOR SIX YEARS WHEN FULTON MAKES A SUPRISING CONFESSION TO HIS WIFE.

INITIALLY MARGE CONSIDERS A DIVORCE. BUT FULTON PLEADS FOR A RECONCILIATION.

MARGE ACCEPTS FULTON'S APOLOGY. TWO YEARS PASS. ONE DAY SHE DECIDES SHE HAS HAD IT WITH FULT.

116

THE NEXT DAY MARGE FILES FOR DIVORCE ON THE GROUNDS OF ADULTERY. IN COURT, FULTON SUCCESSFULLY DEFENDS THE CHARGE OF ADULTERY BY SHOWING THAT MARGE, BY FORGIVING HIM, CONDONED THE AFFAIR. MARGE'S CLAIM FOR DIVORCE IS DENIED.

CASE STUDY II CHILD CARE

BOB IS A 3rd DAY SUFFER'N' JOB'S CARETAKER, WHILE HIS WIFE JERYL IS A MEMBER OF THE CHURCH OF FLANGED FOLLOWERS OF CHIP HUDSON THE DIVINE. THEY HAVE A SON. BOB AND JERYL CANNOT DECIDE BETWEEN THEMSELVES WHICH FAITH THE CHILD SHOULD BE REARED UNTO.

"THE LITTLE SKEETER NEEDS TO KNOW THE TRUTH WHICH ONLY 3rd DAY SUFFER'N' JOB'S CARETAKERS TRULY KNOW."

"GET OFF THAT WACKY CULT GARBAGE. THIS BOY NEEDS TO FIND THE LIGHT THAT ONLY CHIP HUDSON CAN REVEAL."

THE ISSUE GOES TO COURT. SINCE THE LAW CONSIDERS THE FATHER THE PROVIDER AND THEREBY HEAD OF THE HOUSEHOLD, IT IS MOST LIKELY THAT HIS WISHES WILL PREVAIL.

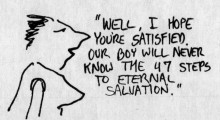

"WELL, I HOPE YOU'RE SATISFIED. OUR BOY WILL NEVER KNOW THE 47 STEPS TO ETERNAL SALVATION."

"AW, CLAM IT."

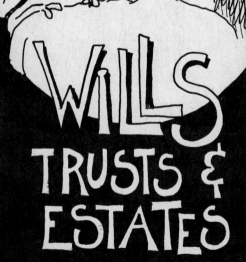

CHAPTER EIGHT

WHEW! SCARED ME... FOR A MINUTE THERE, I THOUGHT YOU WERE FROM THE I.R.S.!

WILLS TRUSTS & ESTATES

WHY A WILL?

IF YOU DON'T LEAVE A VALID WILL, YOU ARE ENTRUSTING THE COURTS AND STATE LAW TO DIVIDE UP YOUR ESTATE. IF THIS IS NOT A DISTURBING THOUGHT, THEN CHANCES ARE YOU'RE PROBABLY ALREADY DEAD.

WILL WORDS

IF LAWYERS CAN DO NOTHING ELSE THEY CAN CERTAINLY COME UP WITH WORDING THAT NO ONE ELSE CAN FIGURE OUT WITHOUT THE AID OF A LAWYER.

INTESTATE

THIS IS NOT A LEGAL HIGHWAY... AN INTESTATE IS A PERSON WHO DIES AND LEAVES NO WILL.

TESTATOR (M) - TESTATRIX (F)

PEOPLE WHO DID THE RIGHT THING AND LEFT BEHIND A VALID WILL ARE GENDER-DENOTED AS TESTATOR (MALE) AND TESTATRIX (FEMALE).

EXECUTOR (M) - EXECUTRIX (F)

"I DIDN'T DO IT..."

THIS UNHAPPY APPELLATION HAS NOTHING TO DO WITH THE TESTATOR'S DEMISE BUT RATHER REFERS TO THE PERSON WHO WILL ADMINISTER, OR EXECUTE, THE WILL.

119

THE ESTATE

"ESTATE" IS A CATCHALL WORD THAT MEANS EVERYTHING THE DECEASED COULDN'T TAKE WITH HIM.

BEQUEST - A SPECIFIC ITEM (OTHER THAN REAL ESTATE) THAT IS IN THE WILL.

LEGACY - ANOTHER WORD FOR BEQUEST.

LEGATEE - SOMEONE WHO GETS A BEQUEST.

DEVISE - A BEQUEST OF REAL ESTATE.

DEVISEE - SOMEONE WHO GETS A DEVISE.

TYPES of WILLS

THERE ARE ALL TYPES OF WILLS, SOME GOOD, SOME BAD AND SOME IN BETWEEN.

THE HOLOGRAPHIC WILL

THIS IS NOT A WILL IN 3-D, SIMPLY A HANDWRITTEN WILL AND SELDOM VALID AT THAT.*

DUCK! THE WILL IS COMING RIGHT AT US!

*UNLESS WITNESSED BY OTHERS.

THE NONCUPATIVE WILL

POPULAR ON THE BATTLEFIELD, WHERE FEW PRACTICING ATTORNEYS DARE PRACTICE, THIS IS THE WILL OF THE SOLDIER, OR OTHERS, WHO ARE ABOUT TO FACE IMMINENT DANGER. THIS IS AN ORAL WILL, SPOKEN TO ANOTHER. IT IS USUALLY VALID BUT NOT FOR LONG. TERMINALLY ILL OR ACCIDENT VICTIMS MAY MAKE VALID NONCUPATIVE WILLS PROVIDED THERE ARE AT LEAST TWO PEOPLE PRESENT.

THE CONDITIONAL WILL

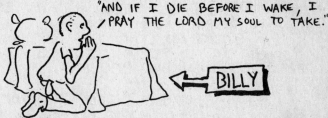

"AND IF I DIE BEFORE I WAKE, I PRAY THE LORD MY SOUL TO TAKE."

← BILLY

STRICTLY SPEAKING, LEGALLY, IF BILLY WERE TO DIE, SAY TOMORROW AFTERNOON, THE LORD WOULD NOT BE UNDER ANY CONTRACTUAL OBLIGATION TO TAKE BILLY'S SOUL SINCE BILLY'S CONDITIONAL WILL PERTAINS ONLY TO BILLY'S SLEEPING STATE... SOMETHING TO KEEP IN MIND WHEN MAKING BED-TIME PRAYERS.

MOST CONDITIONAL WILLS ARE DRAWN UP BY PEOPLE ABOUT TO EMBARK ON A TRIP, AND THE WILL BECOMES INVALID UPON THEIR SAFE RE-TURN.

THE GOOD WILL

ELEMENTS OF A TYPICAL VALID WILL -

1. I, BUD KING, BEING OF SOUND MIND AND STOUT BODY, DO HEREBY DECLARE THE FOLLOWING TO BE MY LAST WILL & TESTAMENT.

2. RIGHT OFF, I DIRECT MY EXECUTOR, HEREINAFTER NAMED, TO PAY MY DEBTS AND FUNERAL EXPENSES AS SOON AS PRACTICAL.

3. NEXT, I WISH MY BODY TO BE CREMATED, AND MY ASHES PLACED IN AN URN AND INTERNED AT ROSEGLUB MAUSOLEUM.

4. NEXT, I DIRECT $10,000.00 OF MY ESTATE TO BE PAID TO MY BARBER, BUD GELP, A GREAT GUY. FURTHER, I DIRECT MY ESTATE TO PAY ANY AND ALL TAXES LEVIED ON THIS BEQUEST.

5. NEXT, I HEREBY DIRECT THAT THE REMAINDER OF MY ESTATE BE PAID TO MY BROTHER, WAYNE KING. FINALLY, I HEREBY NOMINATE MY BROTHER, WAYNE KING, TO BE EXECUTOR UNDER THIS MY LAST WILL AND TESTAMENT.

6. LASTLY, IT IS MY WISH THAT MY EXECUTOR BE FREE FROM PAYING ANY BOND OR OTHER SECURITY FOR THE PERFORMANCE OF HIS DUTIES.

7. IN WITNESS WHEREOF I SIGN AND DATE THIS:

Bud King
SIGNATURE

_11-11-71_
DATE

8. WITNESSED BY:

Jerry Riggs   1214 BOLTBAR RD., LINHOP OH.
Dale Carnogie   4178 DALFLATZ ST., TUB TX.

122

1. WHAT ELSE DO PEOPLE OF SOUND MIND AND BODY DO BUT WRITE THEIR WILLS? IT'S JUST THAT IF SOME DISGRUNTLED HEIR CAN PROVE YOU WERE ON A TWINKIE DIET AND IN SUGAR SHOCK WHEN YOU HAD YOUR WILL DRAWN UP, THEN THERE'S ALWAYS THE CHANCE THAT AN UNHAPPY HEIR WILL WANT TO SEND YOUR WILL AND ESTATE INTO PROBATE, WHERE IT COULD STAY FOR A LONG, LONG TIME.

2. THIS IS A VERY IMPORTANT PART OF THE WILL. YOU MAY THINK THAT JUST BECAUSE THERE'S NO CALL-FORWARDING TO THE HEREAFTER YOU CAN KISS YOUR CREDITORS GOODBYE. NOT TRUE. CREDITORS, LIKE SHARKS AND COCKROACHES, HAVE BEEN AROUND FOR MILLIONS OF YEARS AND WOULD PROBABLY SURVIVE A NUCLEAR ATTACK UNHARMED. AND EVEN IF THEY CANT GET AT YOU IN THE NEXT LIFE THEY CAN CERTAINLY MAKE THINGS UNCOMFORTABLE FOR YOUR HEIRS UNLESS YOU'VE PROVIDED FOR THEM.

3. MOST PEOPLE GO TO THEIR FINAL REST-
ING PLACE IN THE SAME STYLE AS THAT IN
WHICH THEY'VE GONE ALL THROUGH LIFE;
BORING, BORING, BORING. LET'S FACE IT,
THIS IS THE LAST CHANCE ANYONE HAS TO MAKE
THE SIX O'CLOCK NEWS.

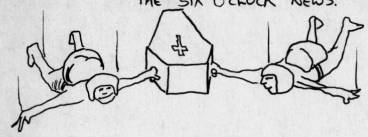

4. THIS IS THE PART OF THE WILL WHERE YOU
CAN LET PEOPLE KNOW WHAT YOU **REALLY**
THOUGHT OF THEM. THIS IS THE ONLY TIME
YOU'LL EVER **REALLY** GET THE LAST WORD.

5. A LOT OF HEREBYS IN A WILL CAN'T
HURT SO LONG AS YOU ACTUALLY GET
AROUND TO NAMING YOUR EXECUTOR
OR EXECUTRIX.

6. AN IMPORTANT CLAUSE, POSSIBLY. MANY STATES REQUIRE THE EXECUTOR TO POST A BOND THAT CAN'T BE CASHED UNTIL THE ESTATE IS SETTLED. UNLESS YOU DON'T TRUST YOUR EXECUTOR, YOU SHOULD HAVE THIS REQUIREMENT WAIVED.

7. DATE IT AND SIGN IT.

8. WHEN YOU SIGN YOUR WILL BE SURE SOME OTHER FOLKS (FRIENDS, FAMILY AND/OR PROFESSIONAL ASSOCIATES) ARE HANDY AND CAN WITNESS IT. WITNESSING SOMEONE'S WILL DOESN'T NECESSARILY MEAN THAT YOU HAVE WITNESSED THE PREPARATION OF THE WILL OR EVEN THE TESTATOR READING THE WILL,

ONLY THAT YOU HAVE WITNESSED THE SIGNING OF THE WILL BY THE TESTATOR.

GOING TO PROBATE

PROBATE IS A JUDICIAL PROCEEDING THAT SEEKS TO ESTABLISH THE VALIDITY OF A WILL. PEOPLE USUALLY TAKE A WILL TO PROBATE BECAUSE THEY WANT TO SEE IT CONTESTED. REASONS FOR CONTESTING A WILL ARE MANY...

FRAUD

JUST LIKE A CONTRACT, A WILL CAN BE INVALIDATED IF FRAUD CAN BE PROVED. ERRORS CAN INVALIDATE A WILL, PARTICUARLY IF THERE IS A WIDE MARGIN BETWEEN WHAT THE ESTATE CLAIMS TO HAVE AND WHAT IT ACTUALLY HAS.

"WHAT DO YOU MEAN, 'DA BUM LEFT ME DE DEED TO DE EMPIRE STATE BUILDING?'"DAT DON'T FIGURE!

UNDUE INFLUENCE

UNDUE INFLUENCE CAN INVALIDATE A WILL, BUT IN ORDER FOR IT TO DO SO IT MUST BE PROVED THAT THE TESTATOR WAS SUSCEPTIBLE (INFIRM, AGED) AND THAT THE BENEFICIARY WAS IN A STRONG POSITION TO EXERT INFLUENCE AND WAS ABLE TO GAIN FROM THAT INFLUENCE.

126

REVOKING A WILL

CANCELING A WILL CAN BE AS SIMPLE AS DESTROYING THE WILL AND ITS COPIES OR IT CAN BE AS COMPLICATED AND FORMAL A PROCESS AS WRITING IT IN THE FIRST PLACE. SIMPLY WRITING "WILL REVOKED" ACROSS THE WILL SHOULD CANCEL IT SO LONG AS IT IS SIGNED AND DATED AND, OF COURSE, PREFERABLY WITNESSED.

LEAVING NO WILL
→ INTESTACY ←

EACH STATE HAS AN ESTABLISHED PROCEDURE FOR DISTRIBUTING THE ESTATE OF A PERSON WHO HAS DIED WITHOUT A WILL. AN ADMINISTRATOR (USUALLY THE NEAREST OF KIN) IS APPOINTED. IF THERE IS NO NEAREST OF KIN OR THE CLOSEST COUSIN IS AS CAPABLE AS A USED KLEENEX...

'AW SHUCKS'

THEN THE STATE PROVIDES THAT THE WIFE AND CHILDREN ARE TO RECEIVE THE PROCEEDS OF THE ESTATE. HOWEVER, EACH STATE HAS DIFFERENT RULES, AND IT IS BEST TO LEAVE A VALID WILL BEHIND.

TRUSTS

A WILL CAN PROVIDE FOR A SPECIFIC GIFT OF PROPERTY AS A BEQUEST OR A DEVISE. A WILL CAN ALSO PROVIDE FOR A TRUST. UNDER A TRUST, LEGAL TITLE TO PROPERTY IS ASSIGNED TO A TRUSTEE WHO IS DIRECTED TO ADMINISTER THE TRUST FOR A BENIFICIARY. TRUSTS CAN WORK SEVERAL WAYS, ACCORDING TO THE DICTATES OF THE WILL. USUALLY, TRUSTS ARE ESTABLISHED FOR CHILDREN...
FOR EXAMPLE:

ONE DAY BOB SOD SR. WAS STRUCK AND KILLED BY A BOLT OF LIGHTNING.

WHEN THE WILL WAS READ, IT WAS LEARNED THAT BOB SOD SR. HAD CREATED A TRUST FOR HIS BABY SON BOB SOD JR.

AS YOUNG BOB SOD JR. GREW HIS TRUST GREW, THANKS TO THE PRUDENT ADMINISTRATION OF HIS MOTHER, WHO WAS THE TRUSTEE.

AT AGE TWENTY-ONE BOB SOD JR. RECEIVED HIS TRUST. THIS WAS TIMELY, AS BOB FACED NEW COMPLICATIONS IN HIS LIFE.

128

ON BEING AN EXECUTOR

WRITING A WILL IS ONE THING, EXECUTING SOME-
ONE ELSE'S IS ANOTHER THING ENTIRELY. AS AN
EXECUTOR, A PERSON HAS THE FOLLOWING
RIGHTS AND RESPONSIBILITIES.

1. TAKE POSSESSION OF ALL PROPERTY
   AND BELONGINGS OF THE ESTATE
   AND ASSESS THEIR VALUE.

2. CONVERT AS MUCH AS
   POSSIBLE OF, OR ALL OF THE
   PROPERTY INTO CASH AND ESTABLISH
   AN ACCOUNT WITH A BANK FOR THE
   ASSETS OF THE ESTATE.

3. ONCE THE ESTATE HAS BEEN VALUED,
   ESTATE TAXES MUST BE PAID. BOTH
   THE STATE AND FEDERAL GOVERNMENT
   REQUIRE PAYMENT OF ESTATE TAXES.

4. AFTER PAYING TAXES, IT'S TIME TO PAY THE OTHER CREDITORS AND THE UNDERTAKER.

"NOW SERVING... #67. THAT'S #67."

5. ONCE ALL THE CREDITORS HAVE BEEN PAID, IT'S TIME TO DISTRIBUTE THE GOODS TO THE BENEFICIARIES AS THE WILL DICTATES.

HELPFUL HINTS

KEEP THOROUGH RECORDS! IF THE ESTATE IS LARGE ENOUGH IT'S A GOOD IDEA TO HIRE A BOOKKEEPER OR EVEN AN ACCOUNTANT. IT IS A DISTINCT POSSIBILITY THAT SOMEONE MAY QUESTION THE ADMINISTRATION OF THE ESTATE. SO, NO MATTER WHO IS OVERSEEING THE BOOKS, SEE TO IT THAT YOUR RECORDS ARE COMPLETE AND ACCURATE.

CHECK THE VALIDITY OF CLAIMS

THE EXECUTOR SHOULD NOTIFY CREDITORS TO COME FORWARD WITH THEIR CLAIMS AGAINST THE ESTATE. ONCE ALL THE CLAIMS ARE IN, IT'S A GOOD IDEA TO CHECK THEM FOR THEIR VALIDITY.

"YEAH, CHECK THIS NAPKIN HERE... HE WROTE HERE HOW HE WAS GOING TO BUY ME A NEW CAR!"

SELLING ASSETS

PROBABLY THE TRICKIEST THING AN EXECUTOR MUST DO IS DETERMINE THE MONETARY VALUE OF THE ESTATE. OF COURSE, THE EASIEST WAY TO DO THIS IS TO CONVERT ALL PROPERTY TO CASH. UNFORTUNATELY THIS MEANS PLACING A CASH VALUE ON IT WHICH MAY BE LOW IN RELATION TO ITS SENTIMENTAL VALUE.

CASE STUDY I

NORMAN PHIF MARRIED EDNA PULP.

"I LOVE YOU."

NOT LONG AFTER THEIR WEDDING DAY NORMAN HAD A WILL DRAWN UP THAT GAVE EDNA EVERYTHING.

"I WANT YOU TO HAVE IT ALL."

THEN THINGS WENT SOUR. THE ONCE HAPPY COUPLE FILED FOR DIVORCE. A PROPERTY SETTLEMENT DETERMINED WHO GOT WHAT.

"EDNA WILL GET THE HOUSE AND THE CAR, NORMAN WILL GET THE TRUST AND THE CONDO."

ONE DAY NORMAN REMARRIED.

"I LOVE YOU"

NORMAN WANTED HIS NEW WIFE TO INHERIT HIS WEALTH SHOULD HE DIE.

"I'LL SEE MY LAWYER IN THE MORNING AND HAVE HIM DRAW UP A NEW WILL."

UNFORTUNATELY, NORMAN DIED THAT NIGHT. HIS ESTATE WENT TO PROBATE. EDNA PRODUCED A COPY OF THE WILL WHICH ENTITLED HER TO EVERYTHING. NORMAN'S RECENT WIDOW CLAIMED THAT NORMAN'S DIVORCE FROM EDNA REVOKED HIS WILL. THE COURT RULED THAT A DIVORCE, IN ITSELF, WOULD NOT REVOKE THE WILL. HOWEVER, SINCE A PROPERTY SETTLEMENT ACCOMPANIED THE DIVORCE THE COURT DETERMINED THAT NORMAN'S WILL WAS NOT VALID AND THAT HIS ESTATE SHOULD BE DISTRIBUTED (AS THOUGH HE HAD NOT LEFT A WILL) TO HIS RECENT WIDOW.

NORMAN PHIF

CASE STUDY II

HOLLIS IS A WEALTHY MAN WITH FEW FRIENDS. HIS GARDEN-ER, CHEN, IS VERY LOYAL TO HOLLIS.

"CHEN, YOU'VE BEEN VERY LOYAL TO ME. I'VE DECIDED TO LEAVE YOU $1,000,000.⁰⁰ WHEN I DIE."

"OH! OK. MR. HORRIS."

UNFORTUNATELY, CHEN DIES JUST DAYS BEFORE HOLLIS. CHEN'S CHILDREN, WHO KNOW OF THE BEQUEST, CLAIM THE $1,000,000.⁰⁰ FROM THE HOLLIS ESTATE.

"GET LOST, SQUIRTS!"

SADLY, THE CHEN CHILDREN HAVE NO CLAIM ON THE MONEY. THIS IS BECAUSE THE FAMILY OF THE BENEFICIARY WHO DIES BEFORE THE TESTATOR CANNOT RECEIVE THE PROPERTY UNLESS THERE IS A SPECIFIC PROVISION TO THIS EFFECT IN THE WILL. THEREFORE, THE ONE MILLION DOLLARS WILL BE DISTRIBUTED ACCORDING TO THE LAWS OF THE STATE AS THOUGH HOLLIS HAD LEFT NO WILL.

CHAPTER NINE

REAL PROPERTY

WHAT IS REAL PROPERTY?

REAL PROPERTY IS LAND AND ELEMENTS THAT ARE A NATURAL PART OF THAT LAND, AND THE ADDED IMPROVEMENTS AND STRUCTURES THAT HAVE BEEN AFFIXED TO THAT LAND.

"DON'T KNOW, HE WAS HERE WHEN WE BOUGHT THE PLACE...AND WELL..."

REAL PROPERTY CAN BE BOUGHT, SOLD, RENTED, USED AS COLLATERAL, INHERITED, TAXED, ZONED AND CONDEMNED. IN THIS CHAPTER, WE'LL LOOK BRIEFLY AT ALL OF THESE POSSIBILITIES AND AT SOME OF THE LEGAL ASPECTS THAT AFFECT THEM.

BUYING & SELLING REAL ESTATE

PEOPLE MAY CHOOSE TO SELL THEIR PROPERTY THEMSELVES OR THEY CAN USE THE SERVICES OF A REAL ESTATE BROKER. THEY CAN AGREE ON A FIXED FEE WITH THE BROKER OR, AS IS MORE OFTEN THE CASE, THEY WILL SIMPLY PAY THE BROKER A COMMISSION BASED ON THE SALE PRICE OF THE PROPERTY. WHEN THE BROKER HAS FOUND A BUYER WHO IS "READY, WILLING AND ABLE" TO BUY, THE BUYER AND SELLER THEN NEGOTIATE A FINAL SALES PRICE ON THE PROPERTY. OFTEN THE BROKER AND SELLER WILL ASK A BUYER TO SIGN A BINDER. SIGNING A BINDER IS RARELY A GOOD IDEA. A SIMPLE DEPOSIT (WITH RECIEPT) IS ENOUGH TO HOLD A PROPERTY UNTIL LAWYERS CAN BE BROUGHT IN TO NEGOTIATE THE SALES CONTRACT.

THE PURCHASE CONTRACT

JUST LIKE ANY OTHER CONTRACT, A REAL ESTATE PUR-
CHASE CONTRACT IS A FORMAL AGREEMENT BETWEEN
TWO PARTIES THAT SPELLS EVERYTHING OUT.
IT CONTAINS THE NAMES OF BOTH BUYER AND
SELLER AND AN ACCURATE, SURVEYED DESCRIPTION
OF THE PROPERTY BEING SOLD. THE CONTRACT LISTS
THE SELLING PRICE OF THE PROPERTY, THE DOWN
PAYMENT MADE AT THE SIGNING OF THE CON-
TRACT AND THE BALANCE DUE UPON TITLE TRANS-
FER. SINCE MOST BUYERS MUST BORROW A LARGE
SUM OF MONEY (CALLED A MORTGAGE) TO BUY THE
PROPERTY, THERE IS USUALLY A CONTINGENCY
CLAUSE THAT INVALIDATES THE CONTRACT SHOULD
THE BUYER BE UNABLE TO SECURE A LOAN.
IF THE BUYER HAS PUT A DEPOSIT DOWN ON THE
HOUSE (AND THIS IS OFTEN REQUIRED), IT'S
USUALLY CONSIDERED A WISE IDEA TO BUY
SOMETHING CALLED "TITLE INSURANCE." TITLE
INSURANCE SIMPLY PROTECTS ANY DOWN PAYMENT
MADE BY THE BUYER SHOULD THE SELLER TURN
OUT TO BE A FRAUD OR THE TITLE TO THE PROPERTY
BE DEFECTIVE OR SHOULD THERE BE ANY
LIENS AGAINST THE PROPERTY.

HOW IT WORKS

1. THE PETERS PUT THEIR HOUSE UP FOR SALE.

— "FOR SALE FOR $50,000.⁰⁰."

2. THE MADISONS WANT TO BUY THE HOUSE BUT DECIDE TO MAKE A COUNTEROFFER.

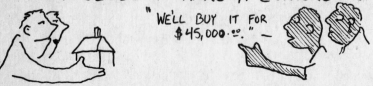

"WE'LL BUY IT FOR $45,000.⁰⁰." —

3. THE PETERS ACCEPT.

"SOLD."

4. THE PETERS ASK THE MADISONS TO SIGN A BINDER ON THE SALE, THE MADISONS WISELY DECLINE. INSTEAD, LAWYERS ARE BROUGHT IN TO WRITE UP A PURCHASE CONTRACT.

5. THE CONTRACT SPELLS EVERYTHING OUT. THIS ALLOWS THE MADISONS A SPECIFIED PERIOD OF TIME TO SECURE A MORTGAGE ON THE PROPERTY. IF A MORTGAGE CANNOT BE SECURED, THE CONTRACT WILL BE TERMINATED. DURING THIS TIME A TITLE SEARCH IS MADE.

6. ASSUMING EVERYTHING GOES WELL — THE MADISONS ARE ABLE TO SECURE A LOAN AND THE PETERS CLEAR ALL LIENS AGAINST THE TITLE — THEN IT IS TIME FOR CLOSING DAY. ON CLOSING DAY, EVERBODY IS THERE. THE PETERS AND THE MADISONS, THEIR RESPECTIVE ATTORNEYS, SOMEONE FROM THE BANK OR MORTGAGE COMPANY AND USUALLY SOMEONE FROM THE TITLE COMPANY. FINALLY, THE BROKER WILL WANT TO BE THERE TO COLLECT HIS COMMISSION.

CLOSING of the TITLE

WHEN THE CONTRACT IS CLOSED, THE TITLE IS TRANSFERRED VIA A DEED. A DEED IS SIMPLY A DOCUMENT THAT DETAILS THE TRANSFER IN WRITING. THE DEED IS THERE TO CERTIFY THAT THE BUYER IS RELEASED FROM ANY UNDISCLOSED CLAIMS OR LIENS AGAINST THE PROPERTY THAT WERE NOT RESOLVED PRIOR TO THE SALE. ANY FUTURE CLAIMS MADE AGAINST THE BUYER FROM PRIOR CONTRACTS CANNOT BE ATTACHED TO THE NEW PROPERTY OWNER BUT MUST BE FORWARDED TO THE FORMER PROPERTY OWNER.

THE MORTGAGE

MOST PEOPLE WHO BUY PROPERTY BORROW A LARGE CHUNK OF MONEY FROM A BANK OR OTHER LENDING INSTITUTION. THE BANK ISSUES A BOND OR PROMISSORY NOTE, WHICH SPELLS OUT THE AMOUNT OF THE LOAN AND WHO MUST PAY IT BACK AND UNDER WHAT TERMS. THE MORTGAGE IS A DOCUMENT THAT PROMISES THAT THE LOAN IS SECURED BY THE VALUE OF THE PROPERTY.

"CONGRATULATIONS, FOLKS, AND THIS HERE IS YOUR 'COUPON BOOK,' OR WHAT YOU MIGHT CALL YOUR REPAYMENT SCHEDULE."

FORECLOSURE

IN THE UNHAPPY EVENT THAT A PROPERTY OWNER CANNOT PAY THE LOAN BACK, THE CREDITOR WHO HOLDS THE MORTGAGE MAY FORECLOSE ON THE PROPERTY. THE FORECLOSED PROPERTY OWNER MAY THEN HAVE TO SELL THE PROPERTY TO PAY OFF THE LOAN.

"OH NO... HA HA... I DON'T WANT TO SELL MY PLACE... I JUST WANT SOMEONE TO TAKE OVER MY MORTGAGE PAYMENTS!"

LEASING-PROPERTY

A PROPERTY OWNER MAY TURN HIS PROPERTY OVER TO ANOTHER WITHOUT GIVING UP HIS TITLE TO THE PROPERTY. THE DOCUMENT THAT SPELLS OUT THIS AGREEMENT IS CALLED A LEASE. THE PAYMENT THE PROPERTY OWNER RECEIVES FOR USE OF HIS PROPERTY IS CALLED RENT.

A LEASE CONTAINS CERTAIN PROVISIONS, WHICH A LANDLORD AND TENANT AGREE TO. IF THE TENANT FAILS TO COMPLY WITH THE TERMS OF THE LEASE, THE LANDLORD MAY TAKE LEGAL ACTION TO TERMINATE IT AND EVICT THE TENANT. OF COURSE, THE TENANT MAY SEE THINGS A LITTLE DIFFERENTLY, IN WHICH CASE A JUDGE MAY HAVE TO ARBITRATE A SETTLEMENT. IN SUCH CASES BOTH TENANT AND LANDLORD HAVE RIGHTS AND OBLIGATIONS. THE ADVISABLE THING TO DO IN SUCH INSTANCES IS TO SEEK OUT THE ADVICE OF AN ATTORNEY WHO SPECIALIZES IN THAT BRANCH OF THE LAW.

144

TENANTS' RIGHTS

AS TIME GOES BY, TENANTS ARE FINDING THAT THEY HAVE MORE AND MORE LEGAL RIGHTS. SHOULD A TENANT HAVE A SPECIFIC GRIPE WITH A LANDLORD, HE IS WELL ADVISED TO CORRESPOND IN WRITING WITH HIS LANDLORD AND TO MAINTAIN A COPY OF ALL SUCH CORRESPONDENCE.

A TENANT WHO DECIDES TO WITHHOLD RENT IS EXPOSING HIMSELF TO THE POSSIBILITY OF EVICTION. HE SHOULD CONTINUE TO MAKE RENT PAYMENTS TO AN ESCROW ACCOUNT OR OTHER THIRD PARTY AS A SIGN THAT HE INTENDS TO PAY IN FULL ONCE HIS DISPUTE WITH HIS LANDLORD HAS BEEN RESOLVED.

CONDO vs CO·OP

TWO BUILDINGS MAY BE OTHERWISE IDENTICAL BUT ONE MAY BE A CONDOMINIUM AND THE OTHER A CO-OPERATIVE. WHEN A PERSON BUYS AN APARTMENT IN A CONDOMINIUM HE TAKES TITLE TO HIS OWN UNIT. IN A COOPERATIVE, A PERSON IS BUYING STOCK OR A SHARE IN THE COMPANY THAT OWNS THE BUILDING. THIS PURCHASE GIVES THE BUYER THE RIGHT TO OCCUPY HIS UNIT. A CONDO OWNER IS RESPONSIBLE FOR SECURING HIS OWN MORTGAGE AND PAYING THE TAXES ASSESSED ON HIS UNIT. A CO-OP OWNER MUST ACCEPT RESPONSIBILITY FOR HIS SHARE OF THE MORTGAGE ON THE ENTIRE BUILDING AND HIS TAXES ARE AGAIN BASED ON HIS SHARE OF TAXES ASSESSED TO THE BUILDING. THEREFORE, A CO-OP OWNER FACES MORE POTENTIAL RISK SINCE HIS RESPONSIBILITY IS AFFECTED BY THE FINANCIAL STABILITY OF THE CO-OP AS A WHOLE. FINALLY THE CO-OP OWNER HAS LESS CONTROL OVER HIS UNIT THAN DOES THE CONDO OWNER. TYPICALLY A CONDO OWNER IS FREE TO SELL OR RENT HIS UNIT AS HE SEES FIT, SINCE HE OWNS HIS UNIT, WHEREAS THE CO-OP OWNER MUST HAVE COOPERATIVE BOARD APPROVAL FOR ANYTHING HE MIGHT DO, EVEN IMPROVEMENTS, ON HIS UNIT.

146

CASE STUDY I

DAL ASKS CLEP TO ACT AS A BROKER TO SELL HIS HOUSE.

DAL TELLS CLEP HE HAS HAD THE PROPERTY APPRAISED AND IT'S VALUED AT $80,000.ºº.

"I WON'T GO LESS THAN, SAY $60,000.ºº"

"BUT TO BE HONEST, THE MARKET IS VERY BAD RIGHT NOW AND I'D BE HAPPY IF YOU COULD JUST GET ITS APPRAISED VALUE."

CLEP FINDS A BUYER WILLING TO BUY THE HOUSE FOR $100,000.ºº

"DEAL" "DEAL"

CLEP OFFERS TO BUY THE HOUSE FROM DAL FOR $75,000.ºº DAL GLADLY ACCEPTS. CLEP THEN TURNS AROUND AND SELLS THE HOUSE TO HIS BUYER FOR $100,000.ºº LATER DAL HEARS OF CLEP'S TREACHERY. HE TAKES CLEP TO COURT AND WINS. CLEP IS ORDERED TO PAY DAL THE DIFFERENCE LESS THE $7,000 (OR 7% COMMISSION) HE WOULD HAVE MADE ON THE SALE.

CASE STUDY II

DAL AND CLEP BURY THE HATCHET. TO SHOW NO HARD FEELINGS, DAL ASKS CLEP TO TRY AND SELL ANOTHER PIECE OF PROPERTY FOR HIM.

"JUST ONE STIPULATION, CLEP, I WON'T TAKE LESS THAN $40,000.ºº ON THIS PLACE."

"GOT-YA."

MONTHS PASS.... THE BEST CLEP CAN DO IS A BUYER WHO IS ONLY WILLING TO PAY $30,000ºº DAL REFUSES.

"SIR I COULDN'T TAKE LESS THAN $40,000.ºº"

"NO DEAL"

DAL INFORMS CLEP THAT HE WANTS TO TAKE THE PROPERTY OFF THE MARKET. SHORTLY THEREAFTER CLEP LEARNS THAT DAL MADE A DEAL WITH CLEPS BUYER TO SELL HIS PROPERTY FOR $30,000.ºº CLEP ASKS DAL FOR HIS COMMISSION. DAL REFUSES. CLEP TAKES DAL TO COURT AND WINS. THE COURT RULES THAT EVEN THOUGH CLEP WAS NOT IN ON THE FINAL SALE, HE HAD LAID THE GROUNDWORK AND THEREFORE WAS ENTITLED TO HIS COMMISSION.

CASE STUDY III

TENANT - LANDLORD

JERBY RENTS AN APARTMENT TO JOE. JERBY AGREES TO PROVIDE HEAT TO JOE'S APARTMENT. DURING THE WINTER MONTHS THE BOILER BREAKS DOWN AND IS NOT IMMEDIATELY FIXED. JOE'S APARTMENT IS COLD. JOE GOES OUT AND BUYS AN ELECTRIC HEATER. HE DEDUCTS THE COST FROM THE RENT.

"FURTHERMORE, I'LL BE DEDUCTING ANY INCREASE IN MY ELECTRIC BILL."

"YOU DO THAT AND I'LL SUE YOU."

IN COURT JERBY IS NOT ABLE TO SUE JOE FOR ANYTHING. LATER THAT MONTH JOE'S FUSE BLOWS. WITHOUT HEAT JOE CONTRACTS PNEUMONIA. JOE DEMANDS THAT JERBY PAY HIS MEDICAL BILLS.

"YOU'RE TO BLAME FOR THIS!"

"SO SUE ME..."

JOE TAKES JERBY TO COURT. JOE IS ABLE TO RECOVER ALL OF HIS MEDICAL COSTS PLUS DAMAGES.

CHAPTER TEN

BUSINESS OWNERSHIP

SOLE PROPRIETOR, PARTNERSHIP, CORPORATION.

WHEN PEOPLE DECIDE TO GO INTO BUSINESS FOR THEMSELVES, THEY HAVE THREE BASIC OPTIONS TO CHOOSE FROM. THEY MAY CHOOSE TO BECOME A SOLE PROPRIETOR, OR THEY MAY JOIN WITH ANOTHER AND FORM A PARTNERSHIP, OR THEY MAY DECIDE TO GO A MORE FORMAL ROUTE AND INCORPORATE. EACH CHOICE PRESENTS ITS ADVANTAGES AND DISADVANTAGES.

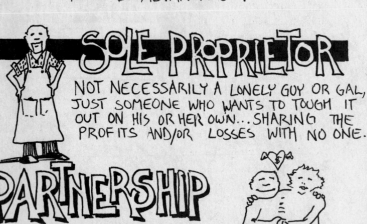

SOLE PROPRIETOR

NOT NECESSARILY A LONELY GUY OR GAL, JUST SOMEONE WHO WANTS TO TOUGH IT OUT ON HIS OR HER OWN... SHARING THE PROFITS AND/OR LOSSES WITH NO ONE.

PARTNERSHIP

PERHAPS MORE MEANINGFUL THAN LOVE IS THE BOND CREATED WHEN TWO OR MORE PEOPLE JOIN TOGETHER TO FORM A PARTNERSHIP.

CORPORATION

CREATED BY ORDINARY PEOPLE, THE CORPORATION IS A LEGAL ENTITY WITH A LIFE ALL ITS OWN.

SOLE PROPRIETOR

A PERSON WHO GOES INTO BUSINESS AS A SOLE PROPRIETOR ASSUMES ALL RESPONSIBILITY (LEGAL & OTHERWISE) FOR THE SUCCESS OR FAILURE OF THE BUSINESS. IF THE BUSINESS FAILS, ITS CREDITORS MAY MAKE CLAIMS ON THE SOLE PROPRIETOR'S PERSONAL PROPERTY. HOWEVER, IF THE BUSINESS SUCCEEDS, THE SOLE PROPRIETOR DOES NOT HAVE TO PAY OUT HIS PROFITS TO ANYONE

THE OTHER IMPORTANT ADVANTAGE IN DOING BUSINESS AS A SOLE PROPRIETOR IS THE SIMPLE AND UNCOMPLICATED WAY OF BOTH STARTING OUT AND CLOSING UP SHOP (SO LONG AS ALL DEBTS HAVE BEEN PAID UP). PROBABLY, THE BIGGEST DISADVANTAGE IS THAT ON A BAD DAY THERE IS NO ONE ELSE TO TAKE THE BLAME.

ASLEEP ON THE JOB AGAIN! HUH! GREAT! LET THE COMPETITION GET A JUMP ON US. WHY SHOULD I CARE? AFTER ALL, YOU'RE THE BOSS.

OH! TODAY I'M THE BOSS? IT SEEMS I'M THE BOSS WHENEVER THINGS ARE GOING BADLY. ALL RIGHT, IF I'M THE BOSS, YOU'RE FIRED!

WHAT? YOU CAN'T FIRE ME!

WHY NOT?

BECAUSE I QUIT!

WHAT? YOU CAN'T QUIT!

WHY NOT?

WELL BECAUSE... UH... YOU'RE UH, WELL YOU'RE VERY GOOD-LOOKING, FOR ONE THING...

FORMING A PARTNERSHIP

WHEN TWO OR MORE PEOPLE DECIDE TO ENTER INTO A BUSINESS RELATIONSHIP, THEY MAY CHOOSE TO FORM A PARTNERSHIP. THE BASIS FOR THE PARTNERSHIP AND THE RIGHTS AND RESPONSIBILITIES OF EACH PARTNER ARE (OR SHOULD BE) SPELLED OUT IN A PARTNERSHIP AGREEMENT.

154

SAMPLE
PARTNERSHIP AGREEMENT

IN ESSENCE, A PARTNERSHIP AGREEMENT IS A CONTRACT THAT SPELLS OUT DUTIES AND OBLIGATIONS FOR ALL PARTNERS.

1. THE PARTNERS ARE JOHN QUIGLET AND PETE MOSS. THE PARTNERSHIP SHALL BE KNOWN AS "QUIGLET-MOSS LANDSCAPE."

2. THE PARTNERSHIP WILL EXIST FROM MARCH 1ST TO OCTOBER 31ST OF THIS YEAR.

3. PARTNERSHIP ASSETS COMPRISE JOHN QUIGLET'S PICK-UP TRUCK, VALUED AT $2500.00, AND PETE MOSS'S LAWN GEAR, VALUED AT $2500.00.

4. BOTH PARTNERS SHALL BE ENGAGED FULL TIME IN THE BUSINESS OF THE PARTNERSHIP.

5. PROFITS AND/OR LOSSES SHALL BE DIVIDED EQUALLY BETWEEN BOTH PARTNERS.

SIGNED	SIGNED

UNFORTUNATELY, FEW PARTNERSHIPS ARE AS SIMPLE AS
THE ONE ON THE PREVIOUS PAGE. MOST INVOLVE
A NUMBER OF PEOPLE BRINGING TOGETHER A VARIETY
OF DISSIMILIAR TALENTS OR CONTRIBUTIONS. IN
SUCH CASES IT IS IMPERATIVE THAT A QUALIFIED
ATTORNEY BE BROUGHT IN TO DRAW UP A SATISFAC-
TORY PARTNERSHIP AGREEMENT.

LIABILITY

GENERALLY SPEAKING, EACH PARTNER IS LIABLE
FOR THAT PORTION OF A LOSS EQUAL TO HIS CON-
TRIBUTION AS A PARTNER. IN CASES SUCH AS FRAUD
OR MALPRACTICE, ALL PARTNERS MAY BE FULLY
LIABLE EVEN IF THEY THEMSELVES CONDUCT
THEIR BUSINESS HONESTLY AND COMPETENTLY.

DISSOLUTION

ANY PARTNER MAY DISSOLVE THE PARTNERSHIP AT ANY
TIME FOR ANY REASON. DEATH AND/OR BANKRUPTCY
OF ONE OF THE PARTNERS WILL ALSO DISSOLVE
THE PARTNERSHIP. A DISSOLVED PARTNERSHIP EXISTS
ONLY TO THE EXTENT THAT ITS AFFAIRS ARE
CLOSED AND ITS ACCOUNTS SETTLED.

LIMITED · PARTNERSHIP

IN A LIMITED PARTNERSHIP THERE ARE TWO
KINDS OF PARTNERS; LIMITED AND GENERAL. A
GENERAL PARTNER IS RESPONSIBLE FOR THE OPER-
ATION AND MANAGEMENT OF THE BUSINESS OF THE
PARTNERSHIP. A LIMITED PARTNER IS PERMITTED
ONLY TO CONTRIBUTE CASH AND/OR PROPERTY TO
THE PARTNERSHIP. HE IS NOT PERMITTED TO ENTER
INTO THE MANAGEMENT OF THE BUSINESS. A GENERAL
PARTNER IS FULLY LIABLE FOR THE ACTIONS HE
TAKES WITH REGARD TO THE PARTNERSHIP, WHERE-
AS THE LIMITED PARTNER IS NOT. THE LIMITED
PARTNER IS LIABLE ONLY TO THE EXTENT HE
HAS AGREED TO INVEST IN THE PARTNERSHIP.

THE CORPORATION

THE THING THAT DISTINGUISHES A CORPORATION FROM AN UNINCORPORATED COMPANY IS THAT A CORPORATION IS A LEGAL ENTITY UNTO ITSELF. WHEN A CORPORATION IS FORMED IN ACCORDANCE WITH THE LAWS OF ITS STATE, IT MAY ENTER INTO CONTRACTS, AND IT WILL ABSOLVE ITS DIRECTORS AND STOCKHOLDERS FROM LIABILITY AND LOSS IN BANKRUPTCY PROCEEDINGS. LASTLY, A CORPORATION CAN CONTINUE TO EXIST LONG AFTER ITS FOUNDERS HAVE PASSED AWAY.

O.K., SO IF WE'RE ALL LEGAL ENTITIES HERE, LET'S CUT BACK AND HAVE A LITTLE FUN.

CORPORATION TYPES

SINCE CORPORATIONS ARE POPULAR, EVERY STATE ALLOWS FOR DIFFERENT TYPES OF CORPORATIONS TO BE CREATED TO FIT CERTAIN SPECIFIC NEEDS. FOR EXAMPLE:

PUBLIC CORP.

THESE CORPORATIONS ARE ESTABLISHED TO SERVE SOME PUBLIC GOOD AND ARE NOT NECESSARILY LOOKING TO MAKE A YEAR-END PROFIT.

MEMBERSHIP CORP.

THESE CORPORATIONS ARE ESTABLISHED BY A SPECIAL-INTEREST GROUP THAT SEEKS TO FURTHER SOME CAUSE OR ACTIVITY (USUALLY RELIGIOUS, CHARITABLE OR SCIENTIFIC). THEY ARE ALSO KNOWN AS "NON-STOCK" CORPORATIONS BECAUSE NO STOCK IS ISSUED; RATHER, THE COMPANY IS SUSTAINED THROUGH MEMBER-SHIP FEES AND DUES.

THE STOCK CORP.

THESE ARE PROFIT-SEEKING CORPORATIONS. OWNERSHIP AND CONTROL OF THESE CORPORA-TIONS DEPEND ON WHO OWNS THE MAJORITY OF STOCK.

THE MAKING

MORE STOCK, IGOR! WE NEED TO ISSUE MORE STOCK!!

OF A STOCK CORPORATION

THE FIRST THING YOU'LL NEED IS A COMPANY NAME. BUT BE CAREFUL, BECAUSE IT CAN'T BE THE NAME OF ANY OTHER CORPORATION IN YOUR STATE. AND IF YOU PLAN TO SELL WARES IN OTHER STATES, YOU'LL HAVE TO MAKE SURE IT'S CLEAR THERE TOO. ONCE YOU'VE FOUND A GOOD NAME, YOU AND YOUR FELLOW INCORPORATORS WILL NEED TO WORD UP A CHARTER. A CHARTER IS A SORT OF WHO, HOW, WHERE AND WHY OF YOUR CORPORATION. EVERY STATE WANTS TO KNOW DIFFERENT THINGS ABOUT YOUR PROPOSED COMPANY, SO THE THING TO DO IS TO CONTACT THE STATE'S SECRETARY OF STATE. IT WOULD ALSO HELP CONSIDER-ABLY TO HIRE AN ATTORNEY.

VENTURE $ CAPITAL

WHEN PEOPLE FORM A CORPORATION, ONE OF THE FIRST ORDERS OF BUSINESS IS RAISING MONEY. TO DO THIS THE INCORPORATORS EITHER SOLICIT THEIR FRIENDS AND ASSOCIATES OR THEY GO PUBLIC. GOING PUBLIC MEANS OFFERING TO SELL STOCK IN THE CORPORATION TO THE GENERAL PUBLIC. STOCK SUBSCRIPTIONS ARE BLOCK PURCHASES OF STOCK MADE EVEN BEFORE THE COMPANY HAS FORMALLY INCORPORATED. INVESTORS WILL DO THIS BECAUSE THEY HAVE CONFIDENCE IN A COMPANY'S MANAGEMENT OR THEY BELIEVE THE COMPANY HAS A PROMISING NEW PRODUCT TO OFFER.

A TALE of TWO STOCKS

A CORPORATION MAY ISSUE TWO TYPES OF STOCK:

1 COMMON STOCK AS ITS NAME

SUGGESTS, THIS IS THE MOST COMMON TYPE OF STOCK ISSUED. IF A PERSON OR GROUP HOLDS 50% OR MORE OF A COMPANY'S STOCK, THEN THEY OWN AND CONTROL THAT COMPANY.

2 PREFERRED STOCK SO NAMED

BECAUSE IF A COMPANY MAKES A PROFIT AT THE END OF THE YEAR, IT MUST PAY ITS PREFERRED STOCKHOLDERS DIVIDENDS FIRST, BEFORE PAYING DIVIDENDS TO COMMON STOCKHOLDERS.

A PERSON WHO HOLDS STOCK IN A CORPORATION OWNS A SHARE OF THAT COMPANY. THIS DOESN'T MEAN A LOT, BUT FOR COMMON STOCKHOLDERS IT DOES MEAN THE RIGHT TO VOTE IN THE ELECTION OF THE COMPANY'S BOARD OF DIRECTORS. IN LARGE CORPORATIONS, STOCKHOLDERS OFTEN TRANSFER THEIR VOTING RIGHTS TO ANOTHER STOCKHOLDER IN WHAT IS CALLED A "PROXY."

THE STOCK MARKET

PEOPLE BUY STOCK IN CORPORATIONS FOR THE DARNEDEST REASONS. MOST OFTEN THEY BELIEVE THAT A PARTICULAR STOCK WILL RISE IN VALUE. ODDLY, THE VALUE OF A COMPANY'S STOCK CAN RISE OR FALL WITHOUT ANY REAL RELATIONSHIP TO HOW WELL THE COMPANY IS DOING. SOMETIMES, A TAKEOVER RUMOR WILL SEND THE PRICE OF A STOCK SOARING. THIS HAPPENS WHEN PEOPLE BELIEVE ONE COMPANY WANTS TO CONTROL ANOTHER BY OWNING A MAJORITY OF THE OTHER'S STOCK. THIS CAUSES THE STOCK TO BE IN DEMAND, SENDING ITS PRICE UP. UNFORTUNATELY, RUMOR CAN BE JUST THAT, AND THE VALUE OF THE STOCK WILL PLUMMET. USUALLY, THOUGH, A COMPANY THAT IS DOING WELL WILL HAVE STOCK THAT RISES IN VALUE OVER THE LONG TERM.

162

DISSOLVING THE CORPORATION

"UH OH". "WHAT SHOULD I TELL THE STOCKHOLDERS?"

END of the LINE.

DISSOLVING A CORPORATION CAN BE MORE DIFFICULT THAN FORMING IT IN THE FIRST PLACE, CERTAINLY A GREAT DEAL MORE DIFFICULT THAN FOR THE SOLE PROPRIETOR WHO WANTS TO THROW IN THE TOWEL. THE PROBLEM WITH DISSOLVING A CORPORATION IS THAT SINCE IT IS A LEGAL ENTITY, APPROVED BY THE SECRETARY OF STATE, THE STATE MUST BE ASSURED THAT THE CORPORATION, WHEN DISSOLVED, HAS SATISFIED ITS DEBTS, RETIRED ITS BONDS AND SETTLED ITS ACCOUNTS.

CASE STUDY I
PARTNER-SHIP

GAB PHLIB   DIT MOLT   CHAUM CHIM   JAD PERKOD

MESSRS. PHLIB, MOLT, CHIM AND PERKOD FORMED A PART-NERSHIP UNDER THE NAME STAFFORD, KLEIN, EVANS AND BROWN. A MAN NAMED F. LEARNED OF THE DISPARITY BETWEEN THE PARTNERS' ACTUAL NAMES AND THE FIRM'S NAMES. HE TOOK THE PARTNERSHIP TO COURT ON THE GROUNDS THAT IT ADOPTED ITS NAME TO MISLEAD THE PUBLIC. F. LOST HIS SUIT.

LEGALLY YOU CAN CALL YOUR COMPANY ANYTHING YOU WANT SO LONG AS IT IS NOT A NAME ALREADY IN BUSINESS OR ONE VERY SIMILIAR TO ONE IN BUSINESS OR THE NAME IS A DELIBERATE ATTEMPT TO MISLEAD THE PUBLIC. IN THIS CASE, THE JUDGE DETERMINED THAT SINCE THE PART-NERS HAD FILED THEIR ACTUAL NAMES WITH THEIR PARTNERSHIP NAMES, THEY HAD ACTED WITHIN THE LAWS OF THE STATE.

CASE STUDY II CORPORATION

MR. BOK, AN INVESTMENT BROKER, WENT ABOUT SETTING UP DUMMY CORPORATIONS AND SELLING STOCK TO NAIVE INVESTORS. ONE INVESTOR, UNHAPPY OVER HIS LOSS, SUED MR. BOK. IN COURT MR. BOK POINTED OUT THAT AS A MEMBER OF THE CORPORATION IN QUESTION HE WAS IMMUNE FROM LIABILITY. THE COURT DISAGREED. WHILE A CORPORATION DOES PROTECT ITS MEMBERS FROM LIABILTY, MR. BOK WAS USING THE CORPORATION AS A CLOAK SPECIFICALLY TO PROTECT HIMSELF FROM PROSECUTION, AND THEREFORE HE WAS LIABLE.

CASE STUDY III CORPORATION

THE STINTS

A MR. STINT ESTABLISHED A CORPORATION IN WHICH HE AND HIS FAMILY MEMBERS WERE THE SOLE STOCKHOLDERS. THE FAMILY CAR WAS TITLED TO THE CORPORATION, THEN LEASED BACK TO THE FAMILY. ONE DAY WHILE DRIVING HOME, MRS. STINT COLLIDED WITH MR. DING'S CAR. MR. DING CLAIMED SUBSTANTIAL INJURIES.

"NECK LASH!"

MR. DING TOOK THE STINT FAMILY TO COURT AND CLAIMED THAT THE CORPORATION WAS A SHELL, THAT THE STINT FAMILY SHOULD BE HELD LIABLE AS THE OWNERS OF THE CAR. THE COURT SAW IT DIFFERENTLY. A CORPORATION IS MEANT TO PROTECT ITS MEMBERS FROM GENERAL LIABILITY.

165

CHAPTER ELEVEN

IDEA

PATENTS, COPYRIGHTS & TRADEMARKS

PATENTS

WHICH CAME FIRST, THE PATENT OR THE INVENTOR? WELL, CERTAINLY THE INVENTIVE MIND HAS ALWAYS BEEN WITH MANKIND.

BUT IT WASN'T UNTIL THE LATE 1700s, WHEN A LEGAL SYSTEM CAME INTO BEING THAT GRANTED PROTECTION AND RIGHTS TO THE INVENTOR, THAT INVENTIONS AND NEW WAYS OF DOING THINGS BEGAN TO CROP UP ALL OVER THE PLACE.

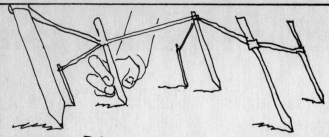

PATENTING AN INVENTION

ANYONE CAN PATENT HIS INVENTION, BUT NOT EVERY INVENTION CAN BE PATENTED; THAT IS, IN ORDER FOR AN IDEA TO BE PATENTED AS AN INVENTION, IT MUST MEET CERTAIN REQUIREMENTS.

1. IS IT USEFUL?

FROM A LEGAL STANDPOINT, A DISCOVERY, IN ITSELF, MEANS NOTHING UNLESS IT CAN SERVE SOME USEFUL PURPOSE, AT WHICH POINT IT IS CONSIDERED AN INVENTION AND CAN BE PATENTED.

2. IS IT NEW?

NATURALLY, IF SOMETHING HAS ALREADY BEEN INVENTED, THE PATENT OFFICE WON'T LET YOU PATENT YOUR OWN VERSION, NO MATTER HOW NICELY YOU ASK, UNLESS YOUR VERSION IS SUBSTANTIALLY DIFFERENT FROM OR BETTER THAN A PREVIOUS DESIGN.

3. IS IT PRACTICAL?

THIS ISN'T TO SAY "USEFUL" AGAIN. IS IT PRACTICAL? IN OTHER WORDS, SOMEONE MAY HAVE AN IDEA FOR AN INVENTION, BUT IF THAT IDEA IS DEPENDENT ON TECHNOLOGY THAT DOESN'T YET EXIST, THEN THE IDEA CANNOT BE PATENTED.

WELL, IT MAY NOT LOOK LIKE MUCH NOW, BUT HOOK IT UP TO A SCORPON HYDROCLAMATOR, WHICH UTILIZES POLYCROMITE SYNTALYSIS, A PROCESS WHICH SOMEONE IS BOUND TO DISCOVER AT SOME POINT IN THE NEXT MILLENNIUM, AND YOU'LL HAVE ONE HELL OF A POWER SOURCE HERE!

GETTING THE PATENT

THE BEST WAY TO GO ABOUT GETTING A PATENT FOR AN INVENTION IS TO HIRE A PATENT ATTORNEY OR AGENT WHO IS QUALIFIED TO REPRESENT YOU AND PREPARE YOUR IDEA FOR A PRESENTATION BEFORE THE PATENT OFFICE.

169

THE PATENT SEARCH

BEFORE YOU SUBMIT YOUR INVENTION, IT IS RECOMMENDED THAT A PATENT SEARCH BE CONDUCTED TO VERIFY THAT THE INVENTION HAS NOT ALREADY BEEN PATENTED EITHER IN THE U.S.A. OR ANOTHER COUNTRY. IF A PATENT SEARCH SHOWS NO PRIOR LIKE INVENTIONS, THEN IT'S TIME TO APPLY FOR A PATENT.

PATENT PENDING

ONCE YOU'VE SUBMITTED YOUR INVENTION TO THE PATENT OFFICE WITH VERIFICATION THAT A PATENT SEARCH HAS SHOWN NO OTHER LIKE INVENTIONS, THEN THE PATENT OFFICE WILL ISSUE "LETTERS PATENT." THESE DO NOT PROTECT THE INVENTOR OR HIS INVENTION PER SE, BUT THEY DO ASSERT THAT THE PATENT IS PENDING AND ALL APPEARS VALID.

INFRINGEMENT

AN UNAUTHORIZED SALE OR MANUFACTURE OF A PATENTED INVENTION IS CALLED AN INFRINGEMENT. AN INVENTOR WHOSE PATENT HAS BEEN INFRINGED MAY TAKE LEGAL ACTION. HE MAY REQUEST AN INJUNCTION TO PREVENT FURTHER SALES AND HE MAY ALSO SUE FOR DAMAGES.

ASSIGNMENTS AND THE INVENTOR

WHEN AN INVENTOR HAS PATENTED AN INVENTION HE MAY ASSIGN OR LICENSE THE RIGHT TO MANUFACTURE AND/OR SELL HIS INVENTION TO ANOTHER. THE INVENTOR MAY SELL THE PATENT RIGHTS OUTRIGHT OR HE MAY ASSIGN THE RIGHTS FOR A SPECIFIC PERIOD OF TIME AND RECEIVE ROYALTIES FROM THEIR PROCEEDS. IF THE INVENTOR ASSIGNS PATENT RIGHTS, IT IS VERY IMPORTANT FOR HIM TO REGISTER THE ASSIGNMENT WITH THE PATENT OFFICE.

"MY INVENTION... THE APRON TIE, AND I WANT TO ASSIGN THE ROYALTIES TO THE SHORT-ORDER COOKS BENEVOLENT SOCIETY."

COPYRIGHTS

WHILE PATENTS PROTECT NEW DEVICES, PROCESSES, ETC., AND THEIR INVENTORS, COPYRIGHTS PROTECT CREATIVE WORKS AND THEIR CREATORS. CREATIVE WORKS INCLUDE PAINTINGS, MOVIES, PLAYS AND MUSICAL COMPOSITIONS. IN ORDER FOR COPYRIGHT PROTECTION TO APPLY, THE CREATIVE WORK MUST EXIST IN SOME FORM (IE., ON PAPER, FILM, CANVAS), NOT MERELY AS AN IDEA IN SOMEONE'S HEAD.

WHAT CAN AND CAN'T BE COPYRIGHTED

CAN

BOOKS, PERIODICALS, LECTURES, MUSICAL COMPOSITIONS, WORKS of ART, MAPS, PHOTOGRAPHS, DRAMATIC WORKS, MOVIES, ILLUSTRATIONS, SCIENTIFIC RENDERINGS.

CAN'T

NAMES, FAMILIAR PHRASES, STANDARDIZED INFORMATION SUCH AS CALENDARS OR GOVERNMENT PUBLICATIONS.

LIBELOUS, OBSCENE OR FRAUDULENT WORKS, IDEAS NOT EXPRESSED IN ANY FORMAL WAY OR MEDIUM.

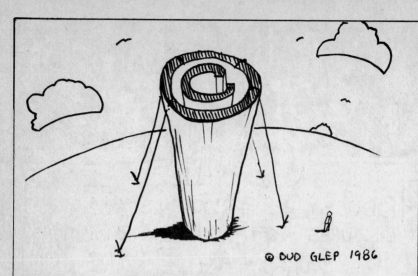

SECURING A COPYRIGHT

© BUD GLEP, 1986

THE FIRST THING TO DO IS TO AFFIX THE COPYRIGHT SYMBOL (© ← "C" IN A CIRCLE) OR THE WORD "COPYRIGHT", WITH THE CREATOR'S NAME AND THE YEAR, SOMEWHERE ON THE CREATIVE WORK. A COPY OR SAMPLE OF THE WORK SHOULD BE SENT IN WITH THE APPROPRIATE FORMS TO THE COPYRIGHT OFFICE IN WASHINGTON D.C.

FAIR USE
OR
HOW TO GET AROUND COPYRIGHT PROTECTION

IT'S NOT ALWAYS MANDATORY TO GET PERMISSION TO USE COPYRIGHTED MATERIAL. THERE IS SOMETHING CALLED "FAIR USE." FAIR USE IS WHAT THE COURTS ALLOW SO THAT REVIEWERS MAY QUOTE SECTIONS OF A COPYRIGHTED BOOK OR TEACHERS MAY INCLUDE COPYRIGHTED MATERIAL IN THEIR LECTURES. BUT FAIR USE RUNS A VERY FINE LINE BETWEEN AUTHORIZED USE AND INFRINGE-MENT.

YOU ARE ON SHAKY GROUND
← FAIR USE
INFRINGEMENT →

INFRINGEMENT

"INFRINGEMENT" IS ANOTHER WORD FOR THEFT. TO PROTECT AGAINST COPYRIGHT INFRINGEMENT, IT IS IMPORTANT NOT ONLY TO INCLUDE THE COPYRIGHT NOTICE ON ALL WORK BUT ALSO TO SUBMIT SAMPLES OF THE COPYRIGHTED MATERIAL WITH APPROPRIATE FORMS AND FEES TO THE COPYRIGHT OFFICE. ONCE A WORK IS PROTECTED, AN INFRINGEMENT SUIT CAN SEEK A COURT INJUNCTION PLUS DAMAGES PLUS PENALTIES FOR ILLEGAL USE OF COPYRIGHTED MATERIALS.

COPYRIGHT PROTECTION

WHEN SOMEONE HOLDS COPYRIGHT TO A PARTICULAR ITEM, HE HOLDS EXCLUSIVE RIGHTS TO THAT ITEM. THESE RIGHTS INCLUDE THE RIGHT TO TRANSFER ONE'S WORK FROM ONE MEDIUM TO ANOTHER. (EXCEPT FROM BOOK TO FILM), THE RIGHT TO TRANSLATE ONE'S WORK INTO A FOREIGN LANGUAGE AND THE RIGHT TO COPY, RECORD AND PERFORM ONE'S WORK. ALSO, COPYRIGHTED MATERIAL IS TRANSFERABLE. THAT IS, THE RIGHTS MAY BE BOUGHT OR SOLD AND USED AS COLLATERAL TO SECURE A LOAN AND MAY EVEN BE BEQUEATHED IN A WILL. THESE RIGHTS ARE PROTECTED FOR THE DURATION OF THE CREATOR'S LIFE PLUS AN ADDITIONAL FIFTY YEARS.*

HOW DO I FIND OUT MORE ABOUT COPYRIGHTS?

CALL THE COPYRIGHT HOTLINE #, (202) 287-9100.

*THIS APPLIES ONLY TO WORK COPYRIGHTED AFTER JANUARY 1st, 1978. WORK COPYRIGHTED BEFORE THIS DATE IS PROTECTED FOR A PERIOD OF 28 YEARS AND MAY BE RENEWED FOR AN ADDITIONAL PERIOD OF 47 YEARS.

TRADEMARKS

THE SYMBOL OR IMAGE THAT A MANUFACTURER AFFIXES TO HIS PRODUCT IS CALLED A TRADEMARK. TRADEMARKS CAN BE REGISTERED WITH, AND PROTECTED BY THE GOVERNMENT. TRADEMARK PROTECTION IS MEANT TO PROTECT BOTH THE MANUFACTURER AND THE CONSUMER FROM RIPOFFS AND CHEAP COPIES.

WAIT A MINUTE. YOU SAY YOU CAN SELL ME THAT $3000.00 WATCH FOR JUST $50.00 BUCKS!!! HOW?

SIMPLE. I BUY DIRECT FROM THE FACTORY AND I DON'T HAVE ANY OVERHEAD.

HMMM... LET ME SEE THAT... SAY, THIS SAYS "ROLEP" NOT "ROLEZ"! THIS IS A RIPOFF!

OH? IT'S NOT THE NAME, IT'S THE WORKMANSHIP... THIS IS JUST AS GOOD.

NO, THANKS.

SNOB!

BEYOND TRADEMARKS

MANUFACTURERS AND OTHERS CAN PROTECT
NOT ONLY THEIR SYMBOL; THEY CAN ALSO
PROTECT THEIR COMPANY NAME. INDUSTRY
GROUPS AND OTHER ASSOCIATIONS OR UNIONS
MAY ALSO PROTECT THEIR NAME AND SYM-
BOL. THESE ARE CALLED COLLECTIVE
MARKS OR CERTIFICATION MARKS, AND
THEY ARE MEANT TO ASSURE CONSUMERS
THAT A PARTICULAR PRODUCT IS, SAY,
AMERICAN-MADE, UNION-MADE AND/OR
MADE OF COTTON.

UNACCEPTABLE MARKS

SYMBOLS THAT CANNOT BE REGISTERED
ARE THOSE MARKS THAT MIGHT BE CON-
SIDERED OBSCENE OR TOO SIMILIAR TO
ANOTHER MARK ALREADY REGISTERED.
ALSO CONSIDERED UNACCEPTABLE ARE
MARKS THAT IMPLY OFFICIAL GOVERN-
MENTAL ENDORSEMENT OR THE ENDORSE-
MENT OF AN AMERICAN PRESIDENT.

CASE STUDY I — PATENTS

MS. TOOP INVENTED A NOVEL WAY TO CLEAN TEETH.

WORKING NIGHT AND DAY, MS. TOOP METICULOUSLY PERFECTED HER DEVICE. SHE DREW UP SCHEMATICS AND FILLED IN ALL THE PROPER FORMS AND SENT IT ALL IN TO THE PATENT OFFICE.

UNFORTUNATELY, THAT VERY SAME DAY A MR. CLOPSTAT DELIVERED TO THE PATENT OFFICE HIS DEVICE—ONE THAT WAS VERY NEARLY THE SAME IN DESIGN AND FUNCTION AS MS. TOOP'S.

OFFICIALS FROM THE PATENT OFFICE REALIZED THAT TWO INVENTORS HAD DELIVERED, ON THE SAME DAY, DEVICES THAT IN ALL CRITICAL ASPECTS, WERE ALIKE. THEY PROPOSED A POSSIBLE SOLUTION TO DETERMINE WHETHER MS. TOOP OR MR. CLOPSTAT SHOULD RECEIVE THE PATENT.

"WHICHEVER ONE OF YOU CAN PROVE THAT YOU HAD THE IDEA FIRST WILL GET THE PATENT."

LUCKILY, FOR MS. TOOP, IN ADDITION TO KEEPING METICULOUS RECORDS SHE ALSO KEPT A DIARY, RECORDING HER EARLIEST HINTS OF THE DEVICE. AS FOR MR. CLOPSTAT, HE COULD ONLY OFFER A VAGUE IDEA OF WHEN HE HIT ON THE CONCEPT AND WHAT HE WAS WEARING.

DEAR DIARY: 1·3·72
FUNNY DREAM LAST NIGHT. MOLAR DECAY AFFLICTING THE NATION. I WONDER DIARY, COULD I HELP? WHAT IF, DIARY, YOU COULD MINITRURIZE A CAR WASH AND PUT IT IN YOUR MOUTH? HMM

CASE STUDY II COPYRIGHTS

A WRITER NAMED QUIG, WHILE YOUNG AND IM-
POVERISHED, WROTE SOME LETTERS TO A FRIEND
NAMED HOAG. YEARS PASSED, QUIG BECAME RICH
AND CELEBRATED AND HIS FRIENDSHIP WITH HOAG
FELL BY THE WAYSIDE. ONE DAY A HISTORIAN
APPROACHED THE LOFTY MR. QUIG.

"I'D LIKE TO DO A
BOOK ON YOUR EARLY
YEARS. GIVE ME ANY
LETTERS OR WRITINGS
YOU HAVE FROM
THAT PERIOD."

QUIG GOT IN TOUCH WITH HOAG AND ASKED FOR
THE LETTERS. HOAG REFUSED. QUIG TOOK HOAG
TO COURT. THE COURT RULED THAT THE LETTERS
THOUGH WRITTEN BY QUIG, WERE RECEIVED BY
HOAG AND REMAINED HIS PROPERTY. MONTHS
LATER HOAG INFORMED QUIG THAT HE WAS
PUBLISHING THE LETTERS IN BOOK FORM,
AGAIN QUIG TOOK HOAG TO COURT. THIS
TIME QUIG WON A RESTRAINING ORDER
WHICH PREVENTED HOAG FROM PUBLISHING
THE LETTERS WITHOUT QUIG'S PERMISSION.
THIS IS BECAUSE THE WRITER OF A LETTER
"OWNS" THE CONTENTS; THE RECIPIENT "OWNS"
THE PHYSICAL LETTER.

ILLUSTRATED
GLOSSARY
OF SELECTED TERMS

ABATEMENT
A QUASHING OR A LESSENING OF A LEGAL PROCEEDING OR ACTION.

ABEYANCE
THE STATE OF BEING PENDING, OR HELD IN SUSPENSION.

AB INITIO
(LATIN) "FROM THE BEGINNING." THE INCEPTION OF A LEGAL RELATIONSHIP.

ACQUITTAL
A FREEING FROM OBLIGATION OR GUILT.

182

ADJUDICATION

A JUDICIAL JUDGMENT;
A DECREE OF BANKRUPTCY.

AFFIDAVIT

A SWORN, WRITTEN STATEMENT.

I swear
* # !

ANNUITY

A PAYMENT OF MONEY MADE
REGULARLY, USUALLY ON AN
ANNUAL BASIS.

ARBITRATION

SUBMISSION OF A DISPUTE BETWEEN TWO
PARTIES TO AN UNBIASED THIRD PARTY.

ARRAIGNMENT

GET UP HERE!

CALLING A PERSON TO COURT SO THAT
HE CAN HEAR THE CHARGES AGAINST
HIM AND RECORD A PLEA.

ARREST

THE DETENTION OF
A PERSON BY LEGAL
AUTHORITY.

ATTACHMENT

THE LEGAL ACT OF SEIZING PERSONS AND/OR PROPERTY.

ATTESTATION of a WILL

THE ACT OF WITNESSING THE EXECUTION OF A WILL.

FIRE!

AWARD

THE GRANTING OF A SUM OF MONEY BY A JUDICIAL BODY TO THE WINNING LITIGANT.

BAIL

SECURITY, USUALLY MONEY, THAT IS SUPPOSED TO GUARANTEE THE APPEARANCE OF AN ACCUSED IN COURT.

GUAR

"TAKE GOOD CARE OF IT."

BAILEE

UNRELATED TO **BAIL**, A BAILEE IS A PERSON ENTRUSTED WITH PROPERTY AS STIPULATED BY THE OWNER.

BENCH WARRANT

AN ARREST ORDER ISSUED BY A COURT.

"ARREST THAT MAN!"

BILL of ATTAINDER

THE PRONOUNCEMENT OF GUILT WITH-OUT BENEFIT OF A TRIAL. NOT PER-MISSIBLE UNDER THE CONSTITUTION.

BILL of LADING

A WRITTEN CONTRACT THAT SPECIFIES A DELIVERY OF GOODS BY FREIGHT.

BILL of PARTICULARS

THE GUY IS A BUM!

A DOCUMENT IN A LAWSUIT THAT AMPLIFIES THE NATURE OF THE COMPLAINT.

BINDER

A TERM THAT INSURANCE AND REAL ESTATE PEOPLE USE, MEANING AN AGREEMENT TO MAKE AN AGREEMENT.

SO WE'RE AGREED, THEN, TO AGREE? AGREED. AGREED.

BONA FIDE

TRUST ME

(LATIN) "IN GOOD FAITH. WITHOUT DECEIT OR FRAUD."

BOND

A CERTIFICATE OF DEBT AS IN "BAIL-BOND," OR AN EXPRESS OBLIGATION OR DUTY.

"I'M DUTY-BOUND, DARLING."

BREACH of the PEACE

DISTURBING THE PEACE.

BRIEF

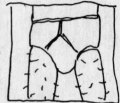

A LITIGANT'S POSITION AS PREPARED BY COUNSEL. NOT TO BE CONFUSED WITH MEN'S UNDERGARMENTS.

BURDEN of PROOF

REQUIREMENT THAT SUFFICIENT PROOF BE OFFERED BY THE ACCUSING PARTY IN A LAWSUIT.

BURGLARY

BREAKING AND ENTERING A HOUSE OR BUILDING WITH INTENT TO COMMIT A CRIME.

CALENDAR

THE LIST OF CASES TO BE TRIED BY A COURT DURING A TERM.

CAPITAL CRIME

A CRIME PUNISHABLE BY DEATH.

CAVEAT EMPTOR

"LET THE BUYER BEWARE."

CAVEAT VENDITOR

"LET THE SELLER BEWARE."

CEASE & DESIST

A REDUNDANT WAY OF SAYING, "CUT IT OUT." USUALLY ISSUED BY A FEDERAL REGULATORY AGENCY TO HALT AN UNFAIR PRACTICE.

CERTIFICATE of INCORPORATION

SORT OF A BIRTH CERTIFICATE FOR CORPORATIONS. ALSO REFERRED TO AS THE "CHARTER."

CHATTEL

ANY AND ALL PERSONAL PROPERTY AND POSSESSIONS EXCEPT LAND.

CIRCUMSTANTIAL EVIDENCE

ALL EVIDENCE THAT SUGGESTS A FACT BUT DOES NOT CONSTITUTE DIRECT PROOF.

CLASS ACTION

A CIVIL CASE WHERE ONE OR MORE LITIGANTS TAKE ACTION ON BEHALF OF THEMSELVES AND OTHERS IN THE CATEGORY OF PEOPLE WRONGED.

CODICIL

A SEPARATE DOCUMENT THAT ATTACHES TO AND MODIFIES A WILL.

COLLUSION

ESSENTIALLY, COLLUSION MEANS THAT TWO OR MORE PEOPLE ARE OUT TO GET YOU BUT YOU DON'T SUSPECT A THING.

COMMON LAW

LAW THAT DERIVED FROM OLDE ENGLISH LAW.

COMMUTATION

A LEGAL MEANS BY WHICH PEOPLE WHO HAVE BEEN CONVICTED OF A CRIME CAN RECEIVE A LIGHTER SENTENCE.

CONDEMNATION

A PERFECTLY LEGAL METHOD BY WHICH PRIVATE PROPERTY CAN BE- COME GOVERNMENT PROPERTY.

CONSPIRACY

A GET-TOGETHER OF TWO OR MORE PERSONS FOR THE PURPOSE OF COMMITTING AN ILLEGAL ACT.

CONTEMPT of COURT

DISRESPECT FOR COURT ROOM DECORUM OR DISOBEDIENCE OF COURT ORDERS.

CONVEYANCE

A DOCUMENT THAT TRANSFERS THE OWNERSHIP OF REAL ESTATE FROM ONE TO ANOTHER.

CORPUS DELICTI

ACTUAL, TANGIBLE EVIDENCE THAT PROVES THAT A CRIME WAS COMMITTED.

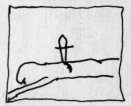

COVENANT

A SPECIFIC PROVISION IN A PROPERTY DEED OR LEASE PERTAINING TO ITS USE.

DAMAGES

COMPENSATION FOR LOSS OR INJURY TO PERSON, PROPERTY OR RIGHTS DUE TO AN UNLAWFUL ACT OF ANOTHER

DAMNUM ABSQUE INJURIA

LATIN, "LOSS WITHOUT INJURY." HARM SUFFERED WITH NO ONE LEGALLY TO BLAME.

DECREE

THE FINAL **WRITTEN** JUDGMENT OF THE COURT.

DEED

THE LEGAL PAPERS THAT TRANSFER OWNERSHIP OF LAND FROM ONE TO ANOTHER.

DE FACTO

AN EXPRESSION USED TO DESCRIBE AN ENTITY OR INDIVIDUAL WHO IS NOT LEGALLY IN POWER.

DE MINIMIS NON CURAT LEX

ANOTHER HANDY LATIN MAXIM, WHICH MEANS THAT THE LAW DOES NOT BOTHER ITSELF WITH SMALL OR TRIFLING MATTERS.

DEFAULT

FAILURE TO APPEAR IN COURT TO DEFEND AGAINST A LAWSUIT.

DEFENDANT

THE DEFENDANT IS THE ACCUSED, IT IS HIS INNOCENCE WE ARE TO PRESUME.

DEMURRER

A WORD AS DIFFICULT TO DEFINE AS IT IS TO PRONOUNCE. ESSENTIALLY, IT MEANS TO ADMIT GUILT YET PLEAD INNOCENCE AT THE SAME TIME.

DEPOSITION

THE TESTIMONY OF A WITNESS WHICH HAS BEEN TAKEN OUTSIDE OF THE COURTROOM BUT STILL UNDER OATH.

DOMICILE

A PERSON'S PERMANENT HOME ADDRESS.

Domicile Sweet Domicile

DUE PROCESS

A↗Z

A CONSTITUTIONAL PROVISO WHICH MEANS THAT NO ONE CAN BE DENIED THEIR RIGHTS WITHOUT ALL FORMAL LEGAL PROCEDURES.

DURESS

EXERTION OF PRESSURE (PHYSICAL OR EMOTIONAL) DESIGNED TO MAKE A PERSON ACT AGAINST HIS OWN BEST INTERESTS.

EASEMENT

THE RIGHT OF A LANDOWNER TO USE THE LAND OF HIS NEIGHBOR FOR NEEDED SERVICES.

EMBEZZLEMENT

THE APPROPRIATION OF PROPERTY BY A PERSON TO WHOM IT WAS ORIGINALLY ENTRUSTED.

ENOCH ARDEN

THE LEGAL MEANS OF DISSOLVING A MARRIAGE WHEN YOUR SPOUSE UPS & VANISHES, NEVER TO RETURN.

ESCHEAT

LATIN, MEANING "TO SNEEZE." ACTUALLY, ESCHEAT IS NEITHER STERNATOLIC IN MEANING NOR LATIN IN ORIGIN. "ESCHEAT" REFERS TO THE REVERSION OF LAND & PROPERTY TO THE STATE WHEN THERE ARE NO HEIRS.

ESCROW

MONEY, ETC. DUE BUT HELD BY A THIRD PARTY UNTIL CERTAIN CONDITIONS HAVE BEEN FULFILLED.

ESTATE

THIS IS EVERYTHING YOU CAN'T TAKE WITH YOU WHEN YOU DIE. IN MOST CASES ESTATE COMES TO MEAN GOVT. PROPERTY IN LIEU OF TAXES.

192

EX POST FACTO

(LATIN) "AFTER THE FACT". NO LAW MAY BE PASSED AND THEN ENFORCED RETROACTIVELY.

EXCEPTION

A WORD LAWYERS BLURT OUT IN THE COURTROOM WHEN THINGS ARE GOING BADLY.

EXECUTOR
(F., EXECUTRIX)

THE PERSON WHO OVERSEES THE DISBURSEMENT OF THE ESTATE AS DIRECTED BY THE WILL.

EXHIBITS

EVIDENCE PRODUCED DURING THE TRIAL THAT IS RELEVANT TO THE CASE.

EXTORTION

OBTAINING PROPERTY ILLEGALLY FROM ANOTHER THROUGH THREATS OF FORCE OR FEAR.

EXTRADITION

IS THE TRANSFER OF A SUSPECTED CRIMINAL FROM ONE STATE TO ANOTHER FOR PROSECUTION.

FELONY

SERIOUS LAW-BREAKING. ALMOST SURE TO GET YOU A SHIRT WITH PERSONALIZED NUMBERS.

FIDUCIARY

BOY SCOUTS ARE TRUSTWORTHY AND BANKERS ARE FIDUCIARY THEY MEAN THE SAME THING.

FIXTURES

PART AND PARCEL TO THE LAND ITSELF. ADDED IMPROVEMENTS TO REAL ESTATE.

FORCE MAJEURE

FRENCH FOR "AN ACT OF GOD."

FORGERY

ALTERING OR WHOLLY MANUFACTURING ANOTHER'S WRITING FOR ONE'S OWN DECEITFUL GAIN.

FRAUD

THE NASTY THINGS THAT PEOPLE DO TO DEPRIVE OTHERS OF THEIR RIGHTS OR OTHERWISE CAUSE INJURY.

GARNISHMENT

AN UNHAPPY STATE OF AFFAIRS WHERE-IN YOUR CREDITORS ARE PAID DIRECTLY BY YOUR EMPLOYER.

GRAND JURY

AN EARLY PHASE OF DUE PROCESS. A GRAND JURY DETERMINES IF THERE IS SUFFICIENT EVIDENCE TO WARRANT A TRIAL.

GUARDIAN

A LEGAL TITLE THAT GIVES A PERSON RESPONSIBILITY FOR THE CARE AND PROTECTION OF A MINOR.

HABEAS CORPUS

A PAPER SERVED ON A JAILER OR SHERIFF TO ASCERTAIN WHY HE HAS TAKEN CUSTODY OF AN INDIVIDUAL.

HEARSAY

FIRST COUSIN TO INNUENDO. HEARSAY IS THIRD-HAND TESTIMONY. NOT MUCH GOOD IN A COURT OF LAW.

HOLOGRAPH

A TYPE OF WILL WRITTEN IN THE HAND OF THE PERSON SIGNING IT.

HOMICIDE

HOMICIDE IS TAKING ANOTHER'S LIFE. IN SOME CASES HOMICIDE IS CONSIDERED JUSTIFIABLE. OTHERWISE IT'S MURDER OR MANSLAUGHTER.

IGNORANTIA LEGIS NEMINEM EXCUSAT

LATIN FOR "IGNORANCE OF THE LAW IS NO EXCUSE."

INDEMNITY

ANOTHER WAY OF SAYING "INSURANCE." INDEMNITY IS THE PROMISE TO REIMBURSE THE LOSS OF ANOTHER.

INDICTMENT

THROW HIM INTO THE IRONS!

IS WHAT THE GRAND JURY APPROVES WHEN IT IS DETERMINED THAT ENOUGH EVIDENCE EXISTS TO TAKE A PERSON TO TRIAL.

HMM?

INQUEST

CONDUCTED BY A CORONER, AN INQUEST SEEKS TO DETERMINE CAUSE OF DEATH.

INTENT

INTERPRETING A PERSON'S INTENT IS LARGELY WHAT LAWYERS ARGUE OVER AND JUDGES MUST DECIDE UPON.

196

INTESTACY

A FIELD DAY FOR LAWYERS.
YOU'RE INTESTATE WHEN YOU DIE WITH-
OUT LEAVING A WILL.

JEOPARDY

THE DANGER YOU'RE IN
WHEN CHARGED WITH A CRIME. YOU
MAY BE CONVICTED AND SENT
TO JAIL.

JUDGMENT

THE FINAL DECISION MADE
BY A COURT OF JUSTICE.

JURISDICTION

THE LEGAL AUTHORITY AND
BOUNDARIES OF A COURT.

LARCENY

AN ILLEGAL ACT WHEREIN ONE
PERSON REMOVES PROPERTY FROM
ANOTHER.

LAST CLEAR CHANCE

WHEN A PERSON DOES NOT CAUSE AN
ACCIDENT BUT MAY HAVE HAD AN
OPPORTUNITY TO PREVENT IT JUST THE SAME,
HE CAN BE LIABLE.

LETTERS OF ADMINISTRATION

GIVE A PERSON AUTHORITY TO ADMINISTER THE ESTATE OF A PERSON WHO HAS DIED INTESTATE.

LETTERS TESTAMENTARY

GIVE A PERSON AUTHORITY TO ADMINISTER THE ESTATE OF A PERSON WHO HAS LEFT A WILL.

LEVY

LEGAL AUTHORITY THAT A COURT HAS TO SEIZE AND SELL THE PROPERTY OF A DEBTOR.

LIBEL

A STATEMENT, MADE IN WRITING, THAT INJURES THE REPUTATION OF ANOTHER.

LIEN

A CLAIM AGAINST ANOTHER'S PROPERTY.

LIS PENDENS

(LATIN) "PENDING SUIT." A WARNING THAT LEGAL ACTION IS TAKING PLACE.

198

MALFEASANCE

PERFORMING AN ACT THAT IS UNLAWFUL AND WRONG.

MALPRACTICE

"NOW WHAT?"

THE LACK OF STANDARD PROFESSIONAL SKILL THAT RESULTS IN AN INJURY TO ANOTHER.

MANSLAUGHTER

"OOPS, HA HA!"

TAKING THE LIFE OF ANOTHER WITHOUT INTENT, AND NOT TO BE CONFUSED WITH A MAN'S LAUGHTER.

MAYHEM

"HEY, GIVE ME MY LEG BACK, YOU MAYHEMER."

DISFIGURING THE BODY OF ANOTHER, USU. TO THE EXTENT OF HAVING SEVERED A LIMB.

MISDEMEANOR

BREAKING A MINOR LAW. DOES NOT OFTEN RESULT IN A PRISON TERM.

MISTRIAL

"YOU MEAN I'M FREE TO KILL AGAIN?"

THE CONCLUSION OF A TRIAL DUE TO A PROCEDURAL ERROR.

199

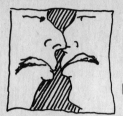

MOOT
A POINT OF DISCUSSION WHICH IS NOT TO BE SETTLED... ONLY ARGUED.

MORTGAGE

A CONTRACT IN WHICH A LOAN IS SECURED THROUGH REAL ESTATE.

MOTION
AN APPLICATION TO THE COURT FOR AN ORDER OR A RECESS.

MOTIVE

THE "WHY" OF CRIME.

MURDER
TAKING THE LIFE OF ANOTHER INTENTIONALLY.

NEGLIGENCE

BEING CARELESS IN A SITUATION WHERE YOU HAVE ASSUMED RESPONSIBILITY.

NOLO CONTENDERE

"WELL, YEAH, KINDA DID IT... I MEAN SORTA, UH, BUT, THE THING IS SEE... WELL YOU JUST GOTTA UNDERSTAND SEE..."

ABOUT AS CLOSE AS YOU CAN GET TO PLEADING GUILTY WITHOUT ACTUALLY CONFESSING FULL GUILT.

NON COMPOS MENTIS

(LATIN) "TO HAVE LOST ONE'S MARBLES... TO BE MISSING AN OAR... NOT ALL THERE... TO HAVE A LOOSE SCREW... NUTS... INSANE..."

NOTARY PUBLIC

A PUBLIC OFFICER EMPOWERED TO ADMINISTER OATHS AND PERFORM OTHER OFFICIAL ACTS.

NOVATION

"YES... BUT WHAT WOULD THEY DO FOR A STANDING NOVATION?"

TWO PARTIES RENEGOTIATE A CONTRACT SUCH THAT THE NEW CONTRACT SUPERSEDES THE OLD.

NUISANCE

AN UNLAWFUL USE OF ONE'S PROPERTY, OR UNLAWFUL PERSONAL CONDUCT THAT IS DEEMED OFFENSIVE.

OATH

"I DO."

SWEARING TO THE SUPREME BEING THAT YOU INTEND TO TELL NOTHING BUT THE TRUTH.

201

OPTION

IN A CONTRACT, AN OPTION ALLOWS ONE OR BOTH PARTIES THE OPPORTUNITY TO TAKE A SPECIFIC ACTION WITHIN A SPECIFIC TIME FRAME.

ORDINANCE

A MUNICIPAL OR LOCAL LAW OR REGULATION.

PARDON

FULL AND FREE RELEASE OF A PRISONER BY THE GOVERNOR OF A STATE.

PAROLE

A CONDITIONAL RELEASE OF A PRISONER FROM HIS SENTENCE.

PARTICEPS CRIMINIS

(LATIN) "AN ACCOMPLICE TO A CRIME."

PARTITION

DETERMINES INDIVIDUAL OWNERSHIP OF PROPERTY THAT IS JOINTLY OWNED.

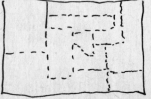

PATENT

THE PROTECTION GIVEN AN INVENTOR BY THE GOVERNMENT FOR A SPECIFIC INVENTION FOR A SPECIFIC PERIOD of TIME.

PERJURY

DELIBERATELY LYING WHILE UNDER OATH. PERJURY IS A CRIME.

PLAGIARISM

A MOST INSINCERE FORM of FLATTERY. PLAGIARISM IS STEALING THE WORK OF ANOTHER.

POWER of ATTORNEY

POSSIBLY THE GREATEST POWER IN THE UNIVERSE. IT GIVES LEGAL AUTHORITY TO ONE TO ACT ON THE BEHALF OF ANOTHER.

PRESUMPTION of INNOCENCE

THE HALLMARK of the LEGAL SYSTEM. THE TENET THAT ALL PERSONS ARE INNOCENT UNTIL PROVEN GUILTY.

PRIMA FACIE

ID LIKE THE PRIMA FACIE, EASY ON THE GARLIC.

THOUGHT BY LAYMEN TO BE AN ITALIAN DISH, BUT ACTUALLY AN EXPRESSION LAWYERS USE WHEN THEY THINK THEY HAVE AN UNBEATABLE CASE.

PROBATE

PROBATE IS TO LAW WHAT ROOT CANAL IS TO DENTISTRY. IT PERTAINS TO WILLS AND ESTATES AND IS USUALLY BEST AVOIDED.

PROBATION

A MEANS BY WHICH A CONVICTED PERSON CAN GO FREE WITH PERIODIC VISITS TO HIS PROBATION OFFICER.

PROCESS

ALL WRITS ISSUED BY A COURT, MOST OFTEN AS IN A SUMMONS, TO CALL A PERSON TO APPEAR.

PROXY

GO TO IT, JACK

IN A CORPORATION A PROXY IS A STOCKHOLDER EMPOWERED BY ANOTHER STOCKHOLDER TO VOTE IN HIS STEAD.

PUTATIVE

DADA?

ACTUALLY I'M JUST YOUR PUTATIVE FATHER.

FOR PATERNITY PURPOSES THE ACKNOWLEDGED FATHER OF AN ILLEGITIMATE CHILD IS KNOWN AS THE PUTATIVE FATHER.

QUANTUM MERUIT

I WANT MORE!

(LATIN) "AMOUNT DESERVED".

THE COURT AWARDS THE PLAINTIFF WHAT HE OUGHT TO GET FOR HIS SERVICES, CONTRACT OR NO.

QUASH

TO ANNUL.

QUORUM

THE MINIMUM NUMBER OF MEMBERS OF AN ORGANIZATION REQUIRED TO BE PRESENT SO THAT A MEETING MAY BE CONDUCTED.

O.K.

RATIFICATION

APPROVAL OR CONFIRMATION.

REAL ESTATE

LAND, AND EVERYTHING GROWING OR BUILT UPON IT.

LET ME AT HIM!

REBUTTAL

EVIDENCE IN COURT OFFERED BY THE PLANTIFF THAT SEEKS TO DISPROVE TESTIMONY OF THE DEFENDANT.

RECEIVER

ONE APPOINTED BY A COURT TO HOLD PROPERTY UNTIL IT'S DECIDED WHAT TO DO WITH IT.

205

RECIDIVIST

A REPEAT OFFENDER.
A CAREER CRIMINAL

REFEREE

A COURT APPOINTEE WHO CAN TAKE TESTIMONY AND HEAR EVIDENCE FROM BOTH SIDES OF A DISPUTE.

GO BACK TO JAIL

REMAND

TO RETURN OR RECOMMIT, AS IN THE CASE OF A PRISONER AFTER HIS HEARING.

REPLEVIN

A LEGAL ACTION, AUTHORIZED BY A COURT, WHICH SEEKS TO RECOVER PROPERTY ILLEGALLY TAKEN.

REPRIEVE

A TEMPORARY SUSPENSION OF THE DEATH SENTENCE.

RES IPSA LOQUITUR

SPEAKING FOR MYSELF...

(LATIN) "THE **THING** SPEAKS FOR ITSELF." IN A LAWSUIT IT WOULD MEAN THAT THE NEGLIGENCE IS VERY OBVIOUS.

EX: FINDING AN EMPTY GIN BOTTLE IN THE DRIVER'S SEAT OF A WRECKED CAR.

206

RES JUDICATA

IS GOING OVER OLD GROUND, THE DETERMINATION THAT A GIVEN DISPUTE HAS ALREADY BEEN SETTLED IN THE PAST.

RESPONDEAT SUPERIOR

THE LEGAL DOCTRINE WHICH CLAIMS THAT AN EMPLOYER IS LIABLE FOR THE ACTIONS OF HIS EMPLOYEES.

ROBBERY

THE CRIME OF TAKING ANOTHER'S PROPERTY BY MEANS OF SOME FORM OF UNFRIENDLY PERSUASION SUCH AS A GUN.

SEQUESTRATION

A COURT ORDER WHEREBY THE SHERIFF TAKES AND HOLDS PROPERTY OF THE DEFENDANT PENDING THE OUTCOME OF A TRIAL.

DID SOMEONE SAY EQUESTRIAN?

PSST

SLANDER

NASTY, POSSIBLY UNTRUE REMARKS THAT ONE MAKES ORALLY ABOUT ANOTHER.

STATUTE

ANY LAW PASSED BY ANY LEGISLATIVE BODY.

"DO THIS!"

"DON'T DO THIS!"

207

STATUTE OF LIMITATIONS

THIS LAW LIMITS THE TIME WITHIN WHICH A PERSON CAN BE ACCUSED AND TRIED OF ANY CRIME.

STIPULATION

AN AGREEMENT.

SUBPOENA

A COURT ORDER THAT REQUIRES THE PRESENCE OF A WITNESS AT A TRIAL.

SUBROGATION

A LEGAL DOCTRINE FOR SUBSTITUTING ONE CREDITOR FOR ANOTHER.

SUMMONS

A NOTICE PRESENTED TO THE NAMED DEFENDANT OF A SUIT. A FIRST STEP IN THE COMMENCEMENT OF LEGAL PROCEEDINGS.

SURETY

SOMEONE WHO PROMISES TO MAKE GOOD THE OBLIGATIONS OF ANOTHER.

SURROGATE

THE JUDGE WHO PRESIDES OVER A COURT THAT ADMINISTERS THE ESTATES OF THOSE WHO HAVE DEPARTED.

TESTAMENT

A PART OF THE WILL. THE DECLARATION OF THE DECEASED AS TO WHO GETS WHAT.

TESTIMONY

EVIDENCE AS OFFERED BY A WITNESS UNDER OATH.

TITLE

DOCUMENTATION ASSERTING THE OWNERSHIP OF PROPERTY.

TORT

A WRONGFUL ACT. ANY CIVIL WRONG WITH THE EXCEPTION OF CONTRACTS AND SMALL FRENCH PASTRIES.

TREASON

BETRAYING ONE'S COUNTRY.

TRESPASS

TO INFRINGE UPON THE PROPERTY OF ANOTHER.

TRUST

THE HOLDING OF PROPERTY BY ONE PERSON FOR THE BENEFIT OF ANOTHER.

ULTRA VIRES

A LATIN TERM THAT REFERS TO AN ACT BY A CORPORATION BEYOND ITS LEGAL AUTHORITY.

UNDERTAKING

A BOND OR OTHER SECURITY NEEDED IN ORDER TO PROCEED WITH A LEGAL ACTION.

UNDUE INFLUENCE

UNFRIENDLY PERSUASION THAT CAUSES A PERSON TO ACT AGAINST HIS WILL AND BETTER JUDGMENT.

USURY

CHARGING INTEREST ON A LOAN WHICH IS HIGHER THAN THE STATE PERMITS.

210

VAGRANCY

A CRIME COMMITED BY THOSE WHO LOSE THEIR HOMES AND JOBS AND WANDER ABOUT.

VENUE

THE PLACE IN WHICH A TRIAL WILL BE HELD. A CHANGE OF VENUE IS SIMPLY A REQUEST TO TRY THE CASE IN A COURT OF A DIFFERENT LOCATION.

VERDICT

THE FINDING OF THE JURY.

VOIDABLE

SOMETHING VALID THAT MAY BECOME VOID THROUGH THE MAGIC OF GOOD LEGAL AID.

VOIR DIRE

IN THE LEGAL PROCESS THIS IS THE RIGHT TO EXAMINE AND QUESTION JURORS BEFORE THEIR SELECTION.

WAIVER

MY RIGHT ARM, MY RIGHT LEG, RIGHT EAR, RIGHT EYE. I'M GIVING THEM ALL UP.

GIVING UP CERTAIN RIGHTS THAT WE ALL HAVE.

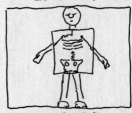

WARRANT

A DOCUMENT THAT THE COURT SIGNS ALLOWING LAW OFFICERS TO COME INTO YOUR HOME, HAVE A LOOK AROUND, AND ARREST YOU.

WRIT

A COURT ORDER REQUIRING A SPECIFIED ACT TO BE PERFORMED BY A DESIGNATED PERSON.

INDEX

MR. MICHAEL HAS CARTOONED
HIS WAY THROUGH SUCH DIVERSE
TOPICS AS ECONOMICS AND
FLYING COWS. CURRENTLY HE
RESIDES IN BROOKLYN.